Douglas County, Colorado:
A Photographic Journey

by
The Castle Rock Writers

Douglas County Court House
Circa 1900

Courtesy Douglas County History Research Center, Douglas County Libraries

Published by The Douglas County Libraries Foundation
100 S Wilcox Street
Castle Rock, CO 80104-1911
303-688-7620
www.douglascountylibraries.org

Printed by:
  Gowdy Printcraft, Colorado Springs, Colorado

Editors:
  Laura Adema
  Alice Aldridge-Dennis
  Susan Koller
  Justine Shaffner
  Lauri Van Court

Project manager:
  Elizabeth Wallace

Historical Editors:
  Shaun Boyd
  Johanna Harden

Special thanks: Burlington Northern Santa Fe Foundation for additional funding of this project.

Front and back covers by Susan Dumler O'Brien using photographs provided by the Douglas County History Research Center, Douglas County Libraries, and the US Forest Service.

Front cover photographs: Douglas County Courthouse, Castle Rock Band and unknown cowboy. Back cover photograph: Elizabeth Dowe.

Douglas County, Colorado

A Photographic Journey

THE CASTLE ROCK WRITERS

Douglas County, Colorado

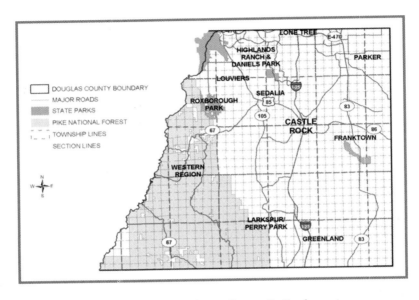

Map Courtesy Douglas County Community Development

Contents

Dedication

We dedicate this book to the memory of Linda M. Grey
(1959– 2004)

Acknowledgements

The Castle Rock Writers wish to thank the following museums, historical societies, foundations and libraries for their help and assistance in the preparation of this book.

American Federation of Human Rights, Co-Masonry, Larkspur, CO; Lucretia Vaile Museum, Palmer Lake, CO; Perry Park Country Club, Larkspur, CO; Castle Rock Museum, Castle Rock, CO; Denver Public Library Western History and Genealogy Department; Colorado Historical Society; Colorado Community Newspapers; Louviers Library and Douglas County History Research Center, Douglas County Libraries; Phil Brook Art Museum, Tulsa, OK; Colorado College, Colorado Springs, CO; *Denver Post*; Larkspur Historical Society; Cherokee Ranch and Castle Foundation, Sedalia, CO; Ann Zugelder Estate, Gunnison, CO; Sedalia Historic Fire House Museum, Sedalia, CO; Louviers Historic Foundation, Louviers, CO; Hagley Museum and Library, Wilmington, DE; Roxborough State Park, Littleton, CO; New Hope Presbyterian Church, Castle Rock, CO; U.S. Forest Service Historical Photograph Collection, NARA, College Park, MD; Mountain Artisans Arts Council, Sedalia, CO; Denver Board of Water Commissioners; Colorado Railroad Museum, Golden, CO, *Castle Rock Daily Star*, Castle Rock, CO.

It is impossible to list each individual with whom our members met as we have collected materials over the last two years. We, the Castle Rock Writers wish to thank everyone in the community who gave so graciously of their time reminiscing, and donating their precious photographs, sketches and letters. We hope you will enjoy our book.

Introduction

Today is so ordinary, so common. We share it with everybody we know. So our new house, our "second-hand" car, our fashionable clothes, our children's Graduation Day pictures, our annual family photos all seem hardly worthy of note.

But, all too soon, today is yesterday. Suddenly, what was common is now rare and strange.

You hold in your hands—the retrieved present—photographs from the past of Douglas County, Colorado. Culled from a variety of sources, the pictures are accompanied by the text of the Castle Rock Writers Group. Under the direction of Elizabeth Wallace, and funded by grants from the Douglas County Libraries Foundation and the Burlington Northern Santa Fe Foundation, these writers dug deeply into the history of their community.

In the process, the authors grew closer not only to their craft, but also to each other. They also grew to recognize the urgent need to capture, preserve and explicate images that were vanishing with remarkable speed. Not long ago, this was a territory of pioneer trails, Front Range ranches and railroad stations. Throughout the 1990s, Douglas County has been the fastest growing region in the United States—an exurban explosion.

The mystery of history is that we never realize we are living in so transient a moment, or how big it really is. Only when that moment is frozen on the page, do we begin to grasp the vast confluence of events that led to that snapshot, that weed in the background, that hat or that smile.

The Douglas County Libraries Foundation and the Burlington Northern Santa Fe Foundation are very pleased to have underwritten this important contribution to our shared memory. The Castle Rock Writers Group is thankful for the opportunity to give back to their community. We are all grateful to the many contributors of photographs and family stories.

It is my personal hope that this book encourages a new generation of readers to explore the richness of their own local past and to savor the history we are creating each instant, right now.

James LaRue
Director, Douglas County Libraries

Chapter One

Castle Rock

County Seat Takes Shape

by
Derald Hoffman

The Rock, Castle Rock, Colo. 1909

The Rock (1909). A southbound train approaches Castle Rock on the Denver & Rio Grande Railroad in this 1909 postcard. To the left of the train can be seen the first Douglas County High School, which was destroyed by fire in 1910. On the far lower right stands the Harris Hotel. Jeremiah Gould, a Rhode Island Civil War veteran, homesteaded the 160 acres south of "The Rock" in 1870. In 1872, the Denver & Rio Grande Railroad made stops in Sedalia and Douglas but did not stop in what is now known as Castle Rock since there was no town or depot and few people in the area. In 1874, the county seat was moved to Castle Rock. Shielded from the worst of the winter storms by the Rocky Mountains, the town was considered an excellent location. Jeremiah Gould donated 120 acres from his homestead. Six streets were laid out, 77 lots were auctioned off for a total of $3,400, and thus, Castle Rock became a town. The following year the Denver & Rio Grande built a rhyolite stone depot in the middle of the town. In 1887, the Atchison Topeka & Santa Fe Railway came through the western part of Castle Rock . *Courtesy Castle Rock Museum.*

Ticket Please (date unknown). The Denver & Rio Grande Railroad Station in Castle Rock became an important center of the community as more people traveled around the country. This independent, narrow gauge line was incorporated in 1870 and facilitated trade from Denver to El Paso, Texas. The first section of the line was finished by the fall of 1871, and soon was picking up freight and passengers in Sedalia, Castle Rock, Larkspur, and Greenland towards the final destination of Colorado Springs. *Courtesy Castle Rock Museum.*

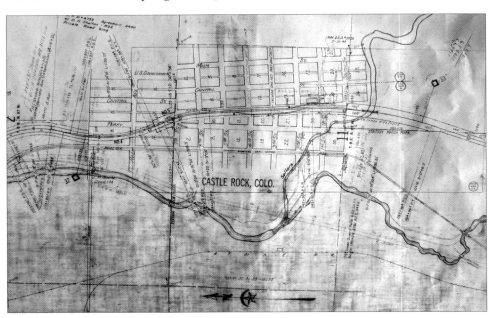

Plotting the Railroad (1919). Pictured above is a Right-of-Way and Track Map for the Denver & Rio Grande Railroad. The Denver & Rio Grande Railroad made runs through downtown Castle Rock east of Plum Creek, and the Atchison Topeka & Santa Fe Railway operated on the west side of Plum Creek. The fast-growing railroads benefited farmers whose produce and livestock could be shipped all over the state. An article in the Castle Rock Journal reports "...good service to the farmer is of the utmost importance when prices and crops in the aggregate are good...." *Courtesy Derald Hoffman from a private collection.*

Take Me Out in Your Surrey With No Fringe on Top. (Circa 1907). This early photograph of the Denver & Rio Grande Railroad Depot shows Mr. E.G. Breselow, stationmaster for the railroad for almost 50 years. He is the man seen center in a white shirt and stationmaster's hat. The Denver & Rio Grande brought in passengers, supplies and mail. It carried lumber from the mills in Larkspur, Sedalia and Greenland, stone from the quarries, coal from the mines, and milk from the dairy farms. The economy prospered -- bringing more families to Castle Rock. *Courtesy Castle Rock Museum.*

Railroad Foreman. (Circa 1928). Mr. & Mrs. Garrigan and their family pose at the back door of the Denver & Rio Grande Railroad Section House. In the front are John and Margaret, daughter Mary is to the right. Mr. Garrigan was section foreman. As foreman, he had to make sure the track was in good condition. Garrigan and his crews checked the rails for any damage in their hand-pump car. A rainstorm might loosen ties, and a solid railroad bed was very important for the safety of the train and the passengers. The journey was uphill from Denver to Monument so the grade had to be constantly maintained. Today, the Union Pacific Railroad maintains the tracks. *Courtesy Castle Rock Museum.*

What a Team! (July 1903). Anna Nelson stands in the doorway of her boarding house at the Douglas Quarry two miles south of Castle Rock. There was much work to be done preparing the meals for hungry quarry miners, cleaning their rooms, washing the linens and sweeping the floors. Her husband, August, was known as "the last of the quarry men". He came from Sweden in 1881 and first worked in the O'Brien quarry where he and Anna set up a boarding house. Silas W. Madge had the most productive stone quarry in the Castle Rock area. Finding lava rock on his ranch in 1872, he slowly began to cut the rock and by 1880 had seventy men working the quarry. The DR&G railroad built a spur to his quarry and the town of Douglas (Castle Rock) thrived. *95048.001 Douglas County History Research Center. Douglas County Libraries.*

The Lion's Share of the Market (Circa 1910). By 1900, The Santa Fe Quarry west of Castle Rock furnished stone for most of the business establishments in the area. A Santa Fe Railway spur facilitated easy removal and transportation of the stone. While Gus Nelson supervised the men in the quarry and Anna ran the boarding house, they were able to save

$4000 and buy the Indian Creek Ranch near Sedalia. Rhyolite was used in the construction of Denver's Union Station, Trinity Methodist Church, as well as many structures in Castle Rock, including the Cantril School. *978011.004 Courtesy Douglas County History Research Center, Douglas County Libraries.*

14

Early Homesteaders (Circa 1885). The Anderson family front row: Jennie, center row (L to R): Elmer, Charles and Louise (mother), back row: Lars (father). The Anderson Family arrived in Douglas County in the spring of 1881. Lars homesteaded land by the railroad tracks near Douglas and worked in the quarries. His son, Elmer, married Olga Decker in 1902, and they had five children. One of the children, John, was the father of Ginny Suelzle, who provided this photograph. Lars and Louise were her great grandparents. *Courtesy Ginny Suelzle, Bothwell, WA.*

Quality Stone (Circa 1900). The architectural firm of W.R. Parsons and Son, of Topeka, Kansas, designed the Douglas County Courthouse at 301 Wilcox Street. The general contractor was J.M. Anderson of Emporia, Kansas. It was completed in July of 1890, but

not before concerned citizens leveled considerable criticism. There were accusations concerning the quality of the rhyolite stone and charges that county commissioners were involved in fraud. No improprieties were proven and the building was completed at a cost of $33,500. The building was placed on the National Register of Historic Places in 1976; unfortunately, the courthouse was destroyed in an arson fire on March 11, 1978. *678001 Courtesy Douglas County History Research Center, Douglas County Libraries.*

An Elegant Building (Circa 1925). A view of Main Street in Castle Rock with cars parked at curbside. The view is looking north from Third Street showing the First National Bank of Douglas County on the far right side of this photograph. It was built in 1904 and was considered one of the most elegant buildings in town. An example of Richardsonian Romanesque - style architecture, it was constructed of rhyolite, and had a roof decorated with cornice brackets and a frieze. *Courtesy Castle Rock Museum.*

Cigars, Honey, Sweets! (Circa 1908). Hally Garfield Johnson named his business "The Sweet Ship." Around 1908, his popular wagon satisfied the sweet tooth of children and adults alike. Johnson sold locally made honey and a variety of candy and tobacco products. Johnson owned the Home Dairy and had considerable trouble with the quality of his dairy products. With the installation of a new boiler and steam sterilizing equipment, he greatly improved the quality of his dairy products. *Courtesy Castle Rock Museum, Betty Saunders Collection.*

Firemen to the Rescue (1923). From left to right: Al Black, Ernest Scott, A.Z. Clark, J.A. Van Lopik, F.B. Rose, George Schweiger, Arthur Dailey, George Hinds, Joseph Bloch, F.A. Curtis, Dallas I. Cox, O.P. Weston, U.S. Sturdevant, George Nickson, J. Grant Hesseltine, H.G. Johnson, Harper McInroy, W.A. Shellabarger, C.E. Huey, E.S. Triplett.

On April 10, 1892, Mayor W.E. Carver was authorized to purchase 300 feet of fire hose at 20 cents a foot. It was to be mounted on a homemade two-wheel cart. Thus began the Castle Rock Fire Department. On April 8, 1896, Ike Satler was appointed Fire Chief and instructed to organize a company of seven men. By June he had purchased caps, belts and blouses. In 1914, the town erected a fire tower and bell; unfortunately, they were destroyed by a cyclone in 1937. Between 1903 and 1915, there were many disastrous fires. A meeting was called January 22, 1915 to mobilize a volunteer fire department. On February 1915, the organization was complete. *Courtesy Colorado Community Newspapers, Copy at Castle Rock Museum.*

Pleasant Memories (date unknown). Rand's Filling Station was located within sight of "The Rock" from which Castle Rock received its name. Mr. Rand also ran a log cabin tourist camp. His Texaco station had a gas pump with an upright, three foot-long handle. Castle Rock resident, Derald Hoffman, recalls similar filling stations. "I remember that one would pull the handle back and forth to fill the large glass container with gasoline. When the gas reached the mark on the glass that indicated the number of gallons, then you would stop and lower the hose and the gas would flow by gravity into your gas tank. The Coke was good, too!" *Courtesy Castle Rock Museum.*

Cool in the Shade (date unknown). Note the cars parked under the spreading cottonwood trees. The view is of Wilcox Street looking north from Third Street. The city fathers valued trees and in 1884 passed a tree-planting ordinance that encouraged local citizens to plant cottonwoods. The ordinance specified tree setbacks and spacing. Trees had to be fenced-in to protect them from roaming cattle. A $10 fine plus court costs was imposed for disturbing ditch flow of water intended for tree irrigation. *98039202 Courtesy Douglas County History Research Center, Douglas County Libraries.*

A Notorious Cafe (2004). The B&B Cafe is well known in the area as a place where people meet, eat, exchange gossip, legal advice and financial assistance. It has been said there was more business accomplished here than at the administration building across the street. In 1880, the first owners, Jack and Edyth Moore had an Italian onyx and marble bar shipped from Leadville, Colorado.

Today upon entering the cafe, patrons appreciate the bar and the tin paneled ceiling with a small hole caused by a gunshot. In 1946, Manuel Perez shot and wounded two Denver police officers. He fled to Castle Rock and hid outside of town for three days. He eventually became hungry and entered the cafe. Locals recognized him, and sent for the marshal. Town Marshal, Ray Lewis, arrived unarmed and attempted to arrest Perez. A struggle occurred during which Perez shot and killed Marshal Lewis. The famous hole in the ceiling is from one of the bullets fired by Perez. At one time, Philip S. Miller, a well-known businessman, opened the Castle Rock Meat Market in what is now the southernmost dining room of the cafe. *Photo Courtesy Derald Hoffman. Information courtesy The Bradley family.*

Rooms for Rent (Circa 1885). Ann Foster purchased the land for this house from William Cantril in 1875. She built the two-story, 15-room home in 1879. It featured an open-coned terraced porch with decorated railings. It became a hotel when David Owens, a New Yorker, converted it, charging from $1.50 to $2.00 a night, a hefty price in those days. A single meal cost 35 cents. A horse barn behind the hotel accommodated visitors' horses. Owens advertised the hotel saying, "Travelers, pleasure and health seekers will find this the prettiest, coziest and neatest house outside of Denver." *Courtesy Castle Rock Museum.*

Businesses Thrive in Castle Rock (Circa 1930). From the beginning of the town in 1874, Perry Street, parallel to the Denver & Rio Grande Railroad tracks, had been the most popular location to own a business, but by 1900 it had shifted to Wilcox Street, one block west, next to Courthouse Square. By then most of the newer business district was between Third and Fourth Streets. Concrete sidewalks were installed in the 1920s. The Du Pont town of Louviers supplied electricity starting in 1921. By 1931 several businesses had added neon lights. *Courtesy Castle Rock Museum.*

A Fire Leads to a New School
(Circa 1890). When the first schoolhouse on "Schoolhouse Hill" burned down in 1896, this facility was used for classrooms until the new school was built. The Holcomb Whitney Hardware Store, located at 321 Jerry Street, included a loading platform and a boomtown false

front. It was subsequently converted to a furniture store and later, after it was damaged by fire, rebuilt and converted to apartments. *678.011 Courtesy Douglas County History Research Center, Douglas County Libraries.*

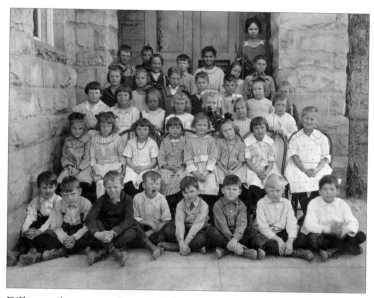

The Cantril School (Circa 1920). Group Front row (L to R) Fred Linklater, Ben Saunders, Joe Hilburger, unknown, Harlan Lowell, unknown, Omer Memmen, unknown. Second row (L to R): Unknown, Mildred Hurlbutt, Dolly Talbott, Evelyn Vosler, Betty Nickson, Jacquiline Moore, Alice Dormer, Thora Pringle. Third row (L to R): Dorothy Dillon, unknown, unknown, Sylvia Hurlbutt, Esther Breselow, Helen Stewart, unknown. Fourth row (L to R): Mildred Flieral, Hazel Webonbuff, George Nixon, Warren Nixon, Delbert Talbott, unknown, unknown, Fifth row (L to R): Fred Rook, Bob Saunders, Theirell Whisenhunt, Edgar Crosswhite, unknown, unknown. *Courtesy Castle Rock Museum.*

An Irishman Settles in Castle Rock (Circa 1898). The Dillon family poses for the camera. (L to R): William, Mary, Elizabeth (mother), Adelaide, Charles, William (father) and Richard. Although William Dillon lived most of his life in Ireland, he arrived on West Plum Creek in July of 1880 from New York. He had a letter of introduction to the Lapham family. Mr. Lapham sent him a mile south to seek room and board at the George Ratcliff Ranch, also known as the T-Ranch. Here he learned to ride horses and once said, "I felt quite comfortable on the back of a reasonably quiet horse, but I never became a bronco-buster." According to William, "Mr. Ratcliff's daughter, Elizabeth, was a real cowgirl." Elizabeth and William were married May 7, 1885, and built a house on Cantril Street. Several years later they moved to Chicago, where William practiced law. Returning to Castle Rock in 1916, the Dillons built a house at 517 Cantril Street. In all, they had 10 children, four of whom died in infancy. *Courtesy Castle Rock Museum.*

Multi-Tasking Family (Date unknown). John Thornley Berry, a dairy farmer, County Commissioner and schoolteacher lived in Douglas County most of his life. He married Grace and together they had four children: George William, John Alan, Ruth Elizabeth and Thomas David. Ruth and Thomas Berry pose with their schoolmates in front of the Cantril School, which was built in 1897. Thomas served in the Navy and, on his release, took a position with the Du Pont Company in Louviers. His wife Evelyn worked for the Social Services in Castle Rock. *Courtesy Castle Rock Museum*

A Victorian Home (2004). The Victorian - style Dyer House is one of the oldest structures in Castle Rock. Located at 208 Cantril Street, it was built by Samuel Dyer in 1875. Dyer was the son of the famous Methodist circuit preacher, Father John Dyer. Dyer was County Clerk and Recorder in 1874. The daily journey from his ranch in Cherry Valley proved too difficult since he had lost his left foot at the Battle of Chancellorsville. He decided to build a home in Castle Rock. In 1880 he married Esther Mary Alexander, widow of Dr. W. J. Alexander. *Courtesy Derald Hoffman.*

From Quarry Owner to Rancher (2004). The Hammar House at 203 Cantril Street illustrates a typical mixture of wood trim and rhyolite construction. Benjamin Hammar, from Cherry Grove, Indiana, married Isabelle Beeson on June 14, 1856. They arrived in the Castle Rock area in 1863. They owned and operated The Castle Rock Stone Company. Hammar was commissioned to construct many buildings in town. A large number of these were built of rhyolite. An excess of injuries at his quarry may have been one of the reasons Hammar took to raising sheep. Threatening letters from ranchers may have also been the reason he and Isabelle moved from the ranch on July 28, 1889. *Courtesy Derald Hoffman.*

For Eternity (2004). Here two lovers lie in a rock tomb. The inscription on Ethel and Laurance's tomb reads: "Within, two lovers lie, together in eternity as they were in life as one." Cedar Hill Cemetery also contains the graves of William Cantril, who built many of the structures in Castle Rock; Benjamin Hammar, a master stonemason; Dr. George Alexander, a family

doctor for over 60 years; and Judge Elias Dyer who was murdered in July 1875 by a vigilante mob in Lake City, Colorado. His father did not want him buried in Lake City, so he brought his body to Cedar Hill Cemetery to be interred. *Courtesy Derald Hoffman.*

Together in Worship (Circa 1910). Before Christ Episcopal Church was built, the Episcopalians met in the J.H. Woltzen's store on the SE corner of Third Street and Wilcox Streets. By 1906, they purchased land on Fourth and Lewis Streets. The new church was finished at a cost of $1700 on April 23, 1907. Bishop Olmstead of Denver consecrated it. Charles Herb, the stonemason, used rhyolite from the Santa Fe Quarry as the primary stone. Rev. James McLaughlin served as the pastor here, at St. Philip In The Field Episcopal Church in Sedalia, and St. Paul Episcopal Church in Littleton. It was 1957 before the church had a full time priest. *678.025 Courtesy Douglas County History and Research Center, Douglas County Libraries.*

The Packing Padres (Circa 1980). German-born stonemason Jean Baptiste Ehmann helped build St. Francis of Assisi Catholic Church in 1888. The church was located on the corner of Third and Jerry Street. Before the church was built, Franciscan fathers from St. Elizabeth's Church in Denver traveled around the county taking enough supplies for Mass and the Sacraments for periods lasting a month. The former church is now the Old Stone Church Restaurant in Castle Rock. *678.101 Courtesy Douglas County History and Research Center, Douglas County Libraries.*

Carpenter and Reverend (Circa 1900). The Castle Rock Methodist Church was built in 1887 and served as a hub for the Methodist Circuit that extended throughout the county. Father John Dyer was an early "circuit rider" minister for the Methodists. When the first lots for Castle Rock were

sold, the "friends of morality" were on the alert and Rev. W.C. Roby, the pastor of the Methodist Episcopal Church, purchased two of the best lots on the corner of Third and Wilcox. The Rev. Todd, a carpenter, helped build this church and therefore was able to keep the price at about $2000. *678024 Douglas County History Research Center, Douglas County Libraries.*

A School Built with Rhyolite (Circa 1914). When the first Castle Rock school burned in 1896, the school board decided to replace the wooden structure with a building constructed of rhyolite stone. The new building opened for classes on September 6, 1897. It was the second building of architectural interest in Castle Rock—besides the courthouse. Cantril School was named after William W. Cantril, an early resident of Douglas County. This building continued to serve grades, 1 through 12, until January 8, 1908, when a new high school was opened at 620 North Wilcox Street. 95048.001 *Courtesy Douglas County History Research Center, Douglas County Libraries.*

Keep Your Horses Outside, Cowboys (Circa 1910). As the Tivoli Saloon, this site was one of the wildest places in Douglas County. Deputies had to keep the cowboys from riding their horses through the saloon. Built by James E. Fetherolf in 1901, of rhyolite stone, it contained 13 rooms upstairs and a saloon on the main floor. It had a ballroom on the second floor where dances were held monthly and on special occasions. The building was renovated in 1930 and renamed the M and N Hotel and Café. It was also known as the Keystone Hotel. Today it is called the Castle Café and is owned by Brad Brown and Tom Walls. 96053 *Courtesy Douglas County History Research Center, Douglas County Libraries.*

Treasurer's Safe Survives Fire (Circa 1930). An interior view of the Douglas County Courthouse in the Treasurer's office, where Fred Linwood Bean is pictured hard at work with his daughter Hattie Elizabeth Bean. Bean served as the County Treasurer from 1923 to 1932. The beloved courthouse building, built in 1889, burned on March 11, 1978. The old black safe pictured in the corner survived the fire. The safe was sold at a closed-bid auction to David A. Curtis of Sedalia for $50. *Courtesy Denna Garcilaso Torres.*

Making Music (1923). Fourteen unknown members of the Castle Rock Band pose outside the courthouse. Castle Rock had its own band as early as 1886. An excerpt in the Castle Rock Journal dated June 7, 1901, reports, "The Castle Rock Band has been reorganized and by industrious practice will be brought up to a high state of perfection by the time of the celebration on the Fourth of July...." Another report in 1923 tells us "...Reverend W.J. Keeser busied himself for several days recently in applying a nice coat of paint to the bandstand in the Court House yard. He applied the paint, which Jim Ranus of the Castle Rock Hardware Store had donated for the purpose. Rev. Keeser did a good job of painting and has the gratitude of the band boys, as well as every other citizen in town for his efforts...the band boys will undoubtedly be thus enabled to make still better music at their regular Saturday night concert." *95048 Courtesy Douglas County History Research Center, Douglas County Libraries.*

Chapter Two

Franktown

The Gardner Legacy

by
Kathleen McCoy and Marjorie Meyerle

Father of Douglas County (Circa 1890). James Frank Gardner, the founder of "Frankstown," was an intellectual who arrived in Douglas County in search of gold.

Failing in that pursuit, he took a job at a local sawmill before going on to become a noteworthy state politician and entrepreneur. He served as Douglas County Clerk and Recorder in 1863, when his property, "The California Ranche," which housed all the county records, was destroyed by fire. He served in the state legislature from 1869-1873 and in the Colorado Senate off and on from 1879-1899, as the County Assessor, Justice of the Peace for Frankstown Township, County Treasurer, and Ute Indian Agent. He was commander of a local 100-day militia, postmaster at Frankstown, and a land speculator in neighboring Castle Rock. Gardner was an acquaintance of Kit Carson, who negotiated with the Arapahoe at Gardner's shingle mill on Cherry Creek in 1862. According to Gardner in Frank Hall's *History of Colorado,* Carson negotiated the release of Ute captives with the leaders of the Arapahoe, threatening war until they relented. Gardner was a friend of Chief Ouray, head of the Ute Nation, who gave him a silver cup that had been a gift to the chief from Ulysses S. Grant. Gardner built a stockade on his property that protected early settlers from hostile Native Americans. The name of Frankstown was ultimately changed to Franktown. *98041.001 Douglas County History Research Center, Douglas County Libraries. (MM)*

Agents of Peace (Circa 1886). According to the Colorado Historical Society, Major Frank Gardner, (second left) the founder of Franktown, and Major Carson (far left) pose outside a stable purported to be the Ouray Agency. Gardner helped to settle the Utes on to their reservation in 1882 and in 1883 was appointed Indian Agent with headquarters at the Ouray Agency in Utah. The Bureau of Indian Affairs merged the Ouray Agency with the Uintah Reservation in 1886, with combined headquarters at Whiterock, Utah. Gardner returned to Douglas County, serving in the Colorado Senate from 1888 to 1892 and the Colorado House from 1896 to 1899. *CHS X7183 Courtesy Colorado Historical Society, Western History Collection. (MM)*

Chief Ouray and Chipeta (Before 1880). The Native Americans resented the onslaught of prospectors because of their occupation of much of the land on the west side of the Continental Divide. The government ordered prospectors to stay away from the areas designated for Native Americans, particularly the Utes, but the prospectors and settlers persisted. By 1860, Ouray had become the chief of the Utes and in his leadership capacity attempted to establish peace between the Utes and the settlers. Since Frank Gardner, father of Franktown, considered Ouray a personal friend, it is likely that Ouray visited the California Ranche in Franktown, although his appearance in Douglas County has not been documented. Throughout their acquaintance, Kit Carson repeatedly advised Ouray to avoid confrontation with the settlers. When the Utes lost much of their land due to shady government negotiations, hostility between the settlers and Utes led to the Meeker Massacre. Ouray was not involved in the Massacre and had always urged peace between the Native Americans and the settlers. Through Ouray's efforts, peace treaties were achieved in 1863, 1868, 1873, and 1880. Respected by Washington officials, Chief Ouray was designated an official spokesman for Indian Affairs in part due to his abilities to proctor peace and the fact that he spoke three languages. Chief Ouray died in 1880 in Ignacio, Colorado. *X-30600 Denver Public Library. (MM)*

Prairie Canyon Ranch Then and Now (Circa 1910). In 1862, German immigrant Frederick Bartruff laid claim to 160 acres of present day Prairie Canyon Ranch. He married neighbor Babette Engl in 1868. The couple continued to improve on the property, despite the burning of their log home and washing away of their barn. The Black Diphtheria Epidemic of 1875 took the lives of Frederick and four of his daughters. Babette married neighboring rancher, John Bihlmeyer, increasing the ranch size to 2,200 acres. The Bartruff cattle brand, connecting J. and R., was registered with the Colorado Territory in 1874. Pictured are John and Babette Bihlmeyer. *93005.046.002 Douglas County History Research Center, Douglas County Libraries. (MM)*

Prairie Canyon Ranch Today Grand Champion (Circa 1980). This magnificent 978-acre property is contiguous to Castlewood Canyon State Park and part of Douglas County's Open Space. In the 1980s, Bob Shultz populated the spread with Texas longhorns and plains bison, and gave the property its present name. Today, registered Red Angus roam the range along with prairie rattlesnakes, pronghorn, elk, Canada geese, thirteen-lined ground squirrels, Woodhouse's toads, blue herons, leopard frogs, badgers, coyotes, and mountain lions. Ancient caves, Native American artifacts, impressive geologic formations, and fossils complete the scenic and anthropological offerings of this unique site. Here Bob Shultz

sits astride *Hopalong Chastity,* the biggest horned steer in 11 states and a state fair grand champion. *Photograph courtesy of Bob Shultz. (MM)*

Settling a Ranch (Circa 1900). The first owner of the land now called Prairie Canyon Ranch was Frederick Bartruff, who homesteaded the first 160 acres in 1862. He built the original log cabin and corrals for his livestock in the protection of a bluff near Cherry Creek. It was unfortunate a family cemetery had to be established in 1875, when Frederick

Bartruff and possibly some young daughters died of the Black Diphtheria. This photo shows buildings the Bihlmeyers added: a barn, sheds, and a calf barn. *93005.006 Douglas County History Research Center, Douglas County Libraries. (KM)*

Homestead Legacy (Circa 1900). This photo of the Bihlmeyer ranch house includes the faces of a homestead legacy. The first owner, Frederick Bartruff was married to Barbara Engle. Her brother, George Engle, assumed ownership of the ranch when Bartruff died. The third owner, John Bihlmeyer, bought it in 1887. John Bihlmeyer married Bartruff's widow, George Engle's sister, Barbara. They had a daughter, who died at about two years of age. Pictured under the tree (L to R): Barbara Engle Bartruff Bihlmeyer, John Bihlmeyer and Katherine Bartruff Seubert, daughter of Frederick and Barbara Engle Bartruff. *90005.004 Douglas County History Research Center, Douglas County Libraries. (KM)*

A Well Trained Horse (1900-1915). After wresting this calf to the ground at the Bartruff-Bihlmeyer-Seubert ranch, it was branded with a hot iron from the fire. A brand can also be applied with a freeze branding, which is done by dipping a copper wire into liquid nitrogen until the temperature drops to 90° below zero. With this method, the pigment cells on the skin, which supply the color, die and the brand emerges white. Notice the role the horse plays in keeping the line taut as the cowboys do their job. The men are unidentified. *93005.012.002 Douglas County History Research Center, Douglas County Libraries. (KM)*

Stacking Hay (1900-1925). In the early 1900s, stacking hay, as it is being done here at the Bartruff-Bihlmeyer-Seubert ranch, could be done with a wooden A-frame having a long boom. A rope runs through pulleys with one end attached to a fork that will lift the loose hay. At the other end, the rope is secured to a vehicle or in this case a horse, which will pull the load up so it can be swung into position. *93005.038.002 Douglas County History Research Center, Douglas County Libraries. (KM)*

Saving Storage and Time (Circa 1900). The hay in this picture is hand stacked in such a way that water would run off, lessening the chance of moisture damage such as mildew. The early homesteaders had to work very hard and many only enjoyed leisure on Sundays. Life got a little easier when the automatic cylindrical baler came into use around 1910. The hay could be baled directly from the windrow, minimizing the loss of nutritional leaves, especially in alfalfa hay. The round baler saved farmers time, labor and storage. *93005.072 Courtesy Douglas County History Research Center, Douglas County Libraries. (KM)*

Cherry School Days (1937). Early schools in the area around Franktown were isolated from each other; they were, however, within easy walking or riding distance of the local residences they served. Students often rode to school horseback and stabled their horses on site. A teacher presided over the school from a raised

platform at the front of the classroom. Students from the various grades mounted the stage to recite their lessons. Outside, existed the horse barn, the boys' and girls' outhouses, and the well. Students drank from a common dipper, were warmed by a potbellied stove, and dabbed their quills in inkwells on wooden desks. Pictured (L to R): Juanita Myers, Vernon Remington, Raymond Dahlberg, Jack Oliver, Russell Mace, Robert Huston, and Wesley Nixon. *654.12 Courtesy Douglas County History Research Center, Douglas County Libraries. (MM)*

A Dedicated Teacher (1862). Miriam Fonder, badly burned in an accident when she was a child, presided over the Fonder School two miles north of Franktown. Here she is with her husband, Hubert, on their wedding day in 1862. Miriam met Hubert when she served as a cook at an Idaho Springs boarding house. When he served in the Civil War, she followed him with her infant as one of four laundresses for his battery. After Hubert was discharged from the Army, they settled on Cherry Creek, where she taught school in her kitchen. After Hubert was kicked to death by a wild horse he was breaking, Miriam and her children kept the farm through blizzards and floods. By all accounts, Miriam Fonder was a tirelessly dedicated teacher who provided an excellent education to her charges. In later years she wrote an autobiography in which she eloquently described the psychic pain her severe disfigurement had caused her, although she claimed she did at last learn to accept it. She lived to be 91. *Courtesy Douglas County History Research Center, Douglas County Libraries. (MM)*

Fonder School (Circa 1980). Hubert Fonder restored a log cabin near his family's property and supplemented it with Indian teepees to house the growing student body south of Parker. In 1884, native Rhyolite stone was hauled by oxen from the Plateau Quarry seven miles west of the site to construct the new school. The Pike's Peak Grange assembly met at the school until it had its own clapboard structure built. An Indian chief in full headdress once interrupted classes at the school when it was taught by Jennie Stone. Accompanied by several braves, he methodically perused a book before departing the fearfully silent classroom. Miss Stone merely continued the day's lesson as if nothing unusual had taken place. *98041.012.001 Courtesy Douglas County History Research Center, Douglas County Libraries. (MM)*

Franktown School Days (Circa 1900). Franktown was the second school district in Douglas County, organized in 1865. It began collecting taxes in 1863. James Frank Gardner donated land for the original school, which began as a log structure and was later remodeled and rebuilt on the site. This building is now part of the

Franktown Fire Department complex and is the current location of the Franktown Historical Society's museum. It holds the distinction of being the oldest public museum in Douglas County. The original school had two chimneys and two classrooms. *645.01 Courtesy, Douglas County History Research Center (MM)*

Multi-functional Building (Circa 1915). This historic structure was once the Franktown Post Office and part of James Frank Gardner's homestead. Later the building was operated as both store and post office with a succession of postmasters and postmistresses  including: Austin Kracaw, Charles Kracaw, Benedict Schutz, and Jessie White. The McLain Family lived here for 19 years, beginning in 1916. Clayton and Ethel McLain conducted one of the largest dairy operations in the area. All but one of their cows were temporarily lost and assumed drowned when the Castlewood Dam broke in 1933. Some were later found, but over half perished. The McLain Family survived the flood, the Dust Bowl Days, the Great Depression, the Grasshopper Pestilence, and drought. *98041.005 Courtesy Douglas County History Research Center, Douglas County Libraries. (MM.)*

Spirited Women (Circa 1910-15). In this photo, Katherine (Bartruff) Seubert is tending cattle on the Bartruff-Bihlmeyer-Seubert ranch. Women were sometimes needed to run the ranch, when men were away on a cattle drive, for instance. Katherine rode as a cowgirl, astride the western saddle in her dress, while her eastern counterparts still rode sidesaddle in long dressy outfits. Cowgirls made history in Colorado as early as 1898, when a group of 200 volunteered to raise a cavalry unit. Though never called up, they showed the capable spirit of ranching women in the west. *93005.045.004 Courtesy Douglas County History Research Center, Douglas County Libraries. (KM)*

Almost a Year in the Making (Circa 1892). The Castlewood Canyon dam was built in 1890, under the direction of A. M. Walles, chief engineer. Its construction created a reservoir for irrigation in the Cherry Creek valley. It took 11 months to build the wall measuring 11 feet thick, 65 feet tall, and 630 feet long. To ensure safety, a second wall was built down stream. Mr. Walles assured the public the dam was built solid to last their lifetime. After three days of heavy rain, it burst August 3, 1933. *92011.003.031 Courtesy Douglas County History Research Center, Douglas County Libraries. (KM)*

Hiking the Dam (Circa 1910). The Castlewood Canyon dam became a recreational attraction for hiking, picnicking, rock climbing and sight seeing. Along the trail were waterfalls, caves and boulders. These folks could have been at the dam in late spring or summer, given the flowers in the lapels and one held on the left. These could have been the pasque flower, a purple, violet or white cup shaped wild flower common in the dam area. Seated on the dam's creek side (L to R): Halley Oltman, Alice Wolfensberger and an unidentified man. *93005.040.003 Courtesy Douglas County History Research Center. Douglas County Libraries. (KM)*

A Leaking Wall (Circa 1892). The Castlewood Canyon dam created a 200-acre lake and was to be used for irrigation. According to Ron Claussen, retired park ranger, these grazing cattle probably belonged to George Engle, who homesteaded in this valley in 1865. As early as May of 1891, the structure and safety of the dam was in question because of leakage. The leakage was severe enough to make water levels too shallow for Engle and other ranchers to irrigate surrounding fields. *92011.003.032 Courtesy Douglas County History Research Center, Douglas County Libraries. (KM)*

CCC. CO. 1845
Camp SCS-7-C Franktown. Castle Rock, Colo. March, 1938.

Enough Work for All (1938). Countless unemployed young men joined the Franklin Roosevelt initiated Civilian Conservation Corps established to put people back to work and to provide job training and civic projects that benefited the local communities. Part of Roosevelt's comprehensive New Deal program to assist the country during a period of economic chaos, the CCC employed three million young men to participate in a peacetime army. Part of its responsibility was soil conservation work and battling erosion. In this effort, it was responsible for planting 3 billion trees in the years from 1933-1942. The CCC also installed telephone lines and helped in various local and national disasters. Here at the Douglas County camp, men from all over the United States came to work on a number of civic projects, including cleaning up the destruction caused by the Castlewood Canyon Dam break in 1933. CCC members retrieved 16 of the McLain dairy cows three miles downstream from the farm. These men worked for weeks, clearing debris and rebuilding fences along Cherry Creek. The national program was closed by an act of Congress in 1942. *98024 Courtesy Douglas County History Research Center, Douglas County Libraries. (MM)*

Goodding Ranch (Date unknown). Typical of many Douglas County ranches of the late nineteenth and early twentieth centuries, family members endured a hardscrabble existence and thus diversified to increase earnings. The Goodding Ranch, formerly the Brackett property, extended along Cherry Creek, fronting the Cherokee Trail, which is now known as State Highway 83. Anna and Samuel Goodding operated a dairy broker business and a farm, cultivating hay, corn, cherries, and apples. The Gooddings also raised pigs, trapped muskrats and coyotes, and sold pelts. *93041.006 Courtesy Douglas County History Research Center, Douglas County Libraries. (MM)*

Frontier Survival and Ingenuity (1946). The Goodding Family and others endured the rupture of Castlewood Canyon Dam, continuous droughts and heavy snowfalls, including a record 38 inches in 1946, as shown. When the Goodding property was owned by Ozro Brackett, it was one of the finest hay ranches in the Divide. Ozro, a stonecutter, built the first Franktown jail and constructed an irrigation ditch that connected W.E. Day's holdings to his own, an enterprise unrivaled by any landowner within 50 miles, allowing the harvest of 200 tons of hay. In 1892, sons, Anson and A.H. Brackett opened the Great Divide Feed Store across from the Denver and Rio Grande Depot in downtown Castle Rock. *98041.013.002 Courtesy Douglas County History Research Center, Douglas County Libraries. (MM)*

The Kelty Family Homestead (Circa 1920). When the Christopher Kelty clan, one of the oldest and most influential Franktown families, arrived by wagon train in 1865, they faced hostile Native Americans. They helped build the fort at California Ranche that provided protection from renegade Native Americans. The family never went on to Washington State, as they had planned. Their offspring helped build the local grange, the fire department and donated part of the land for the historic Franktown Cemetery. Pictured is Harold Kelty on horseback, circa 1920 in front of his 1870 barn and their second, newer barn. *2001.032 Courtesy of Douglas County History Research Center, Douglas County Libraries. (MM)*

Harold Kelty and Friends (Circa 1920). Christopher and Gertrude's descendants continue to live and operate businesses in Franktown, occupying the original homestead houses, built in the late 1860s. Still existing on the original property are a chicken house, and coalhouse from 1872, a calf shed from 1912, a barn, a silo, a garage, and a milk house built in 1900. Here Harold and friends sit outside of the original late 1860s house with its 1880 addition and modernized bay windows. *2001.032.004.003 Courtesy Douglas County History Research Center, Douglas County Libraries. (MM)*

Founder of Russellville (Circa 1870). William Green Russell, in association with his brothers, Levi and Oliver, were the pioneering prospecting family that gave its name to Russellville, just south of Franktown. In 1849, the Russell brothers from Georgia led a prospecting party through the county on their way to the California Gold Rush. After discovering gold particles in washed gravel, they decided to follow Cherry Creek north in search of more. Finding little gold, they continued on to California. In 1858, they returned to Colorado and found gold in Little Dry Creek, starting the Pike's Peak Gold Rush of 1859, which brought many Douglas County settlers to the area, including James Frank Gardner, founder of Franktown. At that time, Russellville was a bustling camp of hundreds of hopeful miners. Unfortunately, there was little gold in the area and various potential prospectors and settlers perished from the cold along the Cherokee Trail. Additionally, an insufficient water supply contributed to the decline of placer mining in the area. The town of Russellville later flourished with a post office, sawmills, a hotel, a blacksmith, and farmers and ranchers of considerable land holdings. For years, Russellville was an important stopping place for travel along the Jimmy Camp Trail or Cherokee Trail, as well as a rest along routes for stagecoaches, freight, and immigrant traffic that continued westward expansion. *CHS 10027505 Courtesy Colorado Historical Society, Western History Collection. (MM)*

Chapter Three

Greenland, Spring Valley and Cherry Valley

Ranchers' Paradise

by
Susan Koller

Small Busy Towns (Circa 1915). An oasis in an area that has often been referred to as the high plains, Greenland was named for its wide-open spaces of inviting rich, green grass. It was originally called Pineland, a name given to the area by the Denver & Rio Grande Railroad in September 1871, but was renamed by the writer, Helen Hunt, who came through the area by train in 1880. Greenland, in the 1930s, was a busy community of about 114 people. It had two stores, a post office, blacksmith shop, garage, school, saloon, and two railroad stations that shipped cattle, potatoes, grain, milk, and cordwood. Spring and Cherry Valleys were smaller communities east of Greenland with ranches dotting the countryside. There were also schools, creameries, and cheese factories established by industrious farmers and ranchers. Spring Valley was a stagecoach stop on the route between Denver and areas farther south. This area in southeastern Douglas County was settled by English, French and German pioneers. Early settlers to Cherry Valley, north of Spring Valley, saw grazing buffalo and a plentiful hunting ground where Native Americans lived and traveled. *Courtesy Larkspur Historical Society.*

Sheep Ranch in Cattle Country (1900-1910). Greenland's rich lands supported the Allis Ranch, pictured here. The Allis Family raised dairy cattle and Hampshire Sheep. Hampshire Sheep came from the south of England and were imported to this country starting in 1865, after the Civil War. This breed was adaptable to most climates and was a good meat producer. Today the ranch and about 148 acres are held in a conservation easement by Douglas County preserving its productive agricultural heritage. *97035.002 Courtesy Douglas County History Research Center, Douglas County Libraries.*

Best of the Best (Circa 1900). A prime example of the Shorthorn breed of cattle is "Villager", a prize-winning bull from the I.J. Noe Ranch west of Greenland. In the 1870s, a change was made to ranches in the area when the "Shorthorns" were brought to Colorado in exchange for the Texas Longhorn cattle. By the time this photo was taken, Douglas County's herds of shorthorns were considered the best in the state. *Courtesy Larkspur Historical Society, Noe Family.*

The Gang's All Here (1894). Pictured here are the students of the Spring Valley School with their teacher, Effie McDowell (seated on the left). All 28 students represent only nine local families. Area family names include McDowell, Smith, Brown, Geiger, Dolan, Bucks, Gandy, Thomas, and Scott. All students' full names are inscribed and numbered on the blackboard in the background along with each student's age. Above the blackboard can be seen a mural which depicts various animals and children. There are also two small groupings of American flags hung just above the children's heads. Most of the children and the teacher are not looking directly at the camera for this group photo, but their attention is focused to the left side of the classroom. The teacher, Effie McDowell, is seated with a note pad in hand. The two boys directly to the teachers left are holding hands. Many of the girls are wearing dresses made of "Apron Gingham," a fabric that was considered finer than the 10 cents a yard calico available at the local store. The school session started in late November and ran through mid-March. Classes resumed after the potato crop was planted in early June and ended in mid September. Tuition for one student was $2.50 a month, with the teacher earning approximately $45 per month. *Courtesy Larkspur Historical Society.*

Ready to Look After Cattle (Circa 1900). Cowboys pictured here from (L to R): Henry Madan, Murray Hall (in photo below also), Pat Dillon, Rick Dillon, and Jay McClure. These men are dressed to look after the cattle, in chaps, hats, "ropes at the ready," with saddlebags, and fresh horses. The much-romanticized cowboy of lore was in reality a hired hand who tended to cattle. *Courtesy Larkspur Historical Society, Wallace Turner Family.*

Cowboy at Play (Circa 1900). This photo reveals two children in the wagon in the background, watching as Murray Hall and his trusty mount show off their skills. There were times to have fun on the ranch as well as work hard. Most ranches of the time were cattle operations, but there were also many horses that needed attention. Branding, cutting out yearlings, ginning, roping, rounding up, and breaking broncos were additional tasks of the Douglas County cowboy. *Courtesy Larkspur Historical Society, Wallace Turner Family.*

Hard Work and Perseverance (Circa 1900). John and Anna (Baker) Geiger strike a typical pose for couples of their day. Their work ethic was also typical of Douglas County pioneers. Mr. Geiger's unsuccessful attempt at prospecting possibly in Russellville turned into a desire to plant roots in Spring Valley. This hardworking couple raised eight children while coordinating the usual activities of a rancher and those of almost any pioneering family such as washing, baking, cooking, soap making, milking, sewing, canning, candle making, preserving meats, and churning butter. It is a wonder the Geiger's had time to pose for their portrait! *Courtesy Larkspur Historical Society, Richard Geiger Family.*

A Ranchers Heaven (Circa 1900). This is the ranch of John and Anna Geiger, the couple in the portrait above. The ranch was homesteaded in 1867. Although only a small snapshot, it provides a glimpse of a typical rancher's day. Notice all the activities going on in the photo. There are at least four people pictured here at various tasks on the ranch. Mr. Geiger had a blacksmith shop; he raised shorthorn cattle and hogs. The Geigers planted orchards and cultivated berry gardens. In addition to building their own home they also built a smoke house, icehouse, gristmill, hay barn, and horse stables. *Courtesy Larkspur Historical Society, Richard Geiger Family.*

The Name Lives On (Circa 1907). Higby Mercantile opened its doors to Greenland consumers July 6, 1907, providing general merchandise as well as selling Model T Fords and gas to "fill 'er up." Higby stocked items local ranchers and farmers could not supply themselves, such as tools, tea, sugar, coffee, fabric, thread, and pots. This store also boasted a root cellar. In 1923, Higby Mercantile was sold to Paul Norwood. To this day, locals who purchased their vegetables and other necessities there remember the Higby name. *Courtesy Larkspur Historical Society.*

A Growing Family (July 23, 1933). This Higby family picnic photo was taken at a reunion in Greenland. John William Higby bought over 1,500 acres in Greenland in 1902. In 1910, he purchased the Greenland Ranch, which was over 16,000 acres. A sawmill was built, and railroad ties for the Denver & Rio Grande Railroad were cut from timber on the property. The Higby sons were involved in all their father's endeavors, helping with the ranch and stores. The family grew in size as well as in its business volume, and the name is still well known in the area. *Courtesy Noe Family.*

A Family Business (1926). This is the family of Paul and Pauline May Norwood; son Dale is on the right, son Roy William on the left. Mr. and Mrs. Norwood purchased the Higby Mercantile in Greenland early in 1923 and managed the general store into 1927 when they sold it. Many people thought that Mr. Norwood ran the store for the Higby's but he in fact purchased the property and ran the business for about five years. When the main road was rerouted and no longer ran through Greenland, the customer base declined, as did the motor traffic. Motorists preferred to travel on a new paved highway, Spruce Mountain Road. This general store catered to area residents with a large range of merchandise from cookies to cigarettes, gasoline to Dutch cleanser, fresh fruit to canned salmon, and crayons to thread. Customers included the school district and familiar family names such as Noe, Best and Quick. *2001.034 Courtesy Douglas County History Research Center, Douglas County Libraries.*

A Pleasure Trip (1895-1900). Mr. Frank Clingman is ready to drive his pleasure buggy, pulled by a Standardbred horse. Standardbred horses are generally regarded the world over as the fastest harness horses. His buggy, often used in place of the everyday wagon, was far more pleasurable to drive because of its stylish appearance and lighter weight.

Dressed up in his formal attire, Mr. Clingman could have been on his way to church, a meeting or other social occasion. *2000.19.2 Courtesy Douglas County History Research Center, Douglas County Libraries.*

4-H Educates Future Ranchers (Circa 1918). The Noe boys, Fred, Charles and Frankie, are pictured with their sheep at the Eagle Mountain Ranch, located just west of Greenland. Their father, I.J. Noe, owned the ranch, and the boys are involved in a 4-H project. Forty-seven of the 48 states in the Union had 4-H clubs in 1918. Participating in a 4-H club was popular; having sheep on a cattle ranch was not. The education provided by 4-H made working with sheep more acceptable to parents who were cattle ranchers. *Courtesy Noe Family.*

Industrious Dairy Farmers (Circa 1900). Taking milk to the cheese factory and creamery was a common occurrence all across the Douglas County. The money made from dairy products provided extra income for a farmer between harvests. The protein-rich grasses and favorable Colorado climate had a prosperous effect on the dairy industry. All were ideal conditions to start a dairy farm. In the late 1870s, dairying was the largest industry and king in Douglas County. *Courtesy Larkspur Historical Society, Wallace Turner Family.*

The Cream of the Crop (Circa 1900). The Spring Valley Creamery started operations in 1894, and was characteristic of creameries throughout the county. Many dairy farmers raised Milking Shorthorn cattle because of their ability to stand up to harsh winters and their capacity to render more butterfat. This breed was introduced to the United States in 1783 and produced the tasty dairy products that made local creameries and farmers like James Pettigrew (L) and his good friend Patrick Murphy (R) successful. *Courtesy Lucretia Vaile Museum.*

An Irish Walker
(Date unknown).
Patrick Murphy,
also known as
"Irish Pat Murphy,"
homesteaded land
in the Spring Valley
area in 1870. He
constructed this log
cabin just across the
El Paso County line.
An early pioneer of
the area, he was
known for walking
almost everywhere.
The cabin was
made with the
steeple notching
method, requiring the log tops be formed into a ridge with a bottom groove. When the
two parts were united, they made a stable joint that allowed Douglas County pioneers fast
and easy construction of their homes. *Courtesy Lucretia Vaile Museum.*

Fun in the Country
(Circa 1910). Mr.
Fred Geiger and
Miss Julia Wiscomb
of Spring Valley
make a handsome
couple; they are
likely out for a
good time maybe
going to the local
dance. Mr. Geiger
was well known for
his love of practical
jokes and his
dancing ability.
Many communities
of the time
announced an
upcoming social event in the local paper. The events included barn dances, Grange events,
schoolhouse get-togethers, box socials. Many times orchestras and refreshments were
added to make a fun event. *95056.014.002 Courtesy Douglas County History Research Center, Douglas
County Libraries.*

That's Greek to Me (1997). The word silo derives from the Greek word "siros." A silo is a place to store silage out of the weather and keep it from further fermentation. This wood silo is on the Ruth Lorraine Ranch in Spring Valley, the date it was built is unknown but the family purchased the ranch in 1905. Notice the beautiful wood joinery of this uncommon wooden silo. Early silos were usually made of wood, but a wooden stave silo commonly had vertical staves not the horizontal staves pictured here. *Courtesy Larkspur Historical Society.*

A Bucket Full of Gas, Please! (1980) Prior to the invention of the gas pump in 1905, one could only purchase gasoline by the bucketful at the local store or repair shop. Early automobile owners usually purchased just enough gas for a single Sunday afternoon pleasure trip, and ranchers went to town for their gas. As ranching became more mechanized, trips to town for gas would have been inconvenient for busy ranchers in remote areas. A pump on the property, such as the one pictured, would have been highly valued. The 1920s pump shown is another one of the unique structures on the Ruth Lorraine Ranch. *Courtesy Larkspur Historical Society.*

Enterprising Marriage (1922). Malrie and Lucy "Carrie" (Ingalls) Taylor are lovingly posed here, possibly right after they were married or on the day itself. The Taylor family consisted of three natural sons and one foster son. Mr. and Mrs. Taylor lived in Greenland for the greater part of their lives. The 1920 census gives the population of Greenland as being about 128 citizens. The population declined as the years passed and now the Greenland area is part of Douglas County Open Space. *Courtesy Larkspur Historical Society.*

It's All in the Family (Circa 1926). This photo shows the Taylors' garage in Greenland. Mrs. Taylor's relations James and Laura Ingalls are pictured here holding the Taylors' son Milton, dating this photo to about 1926. Mr. Malrie Taylor was a very enterprising young man who opened several

businesses in Greenland, which included this garage, a filling station and a restaurant. Mrs. Taylor, who helped her husband with his businesses, also worked as Postmistress in the town of Greenland for 27 years. *Courtesy Larkspur Historical Society.*

Accidental Death (Circa 1890). This house was the home of David Tintle and his wife Julia Alderman; it was built before their marriage on December 12, 1881, in the Cherry Valley area of Southeastern Douglas County. The house is built in the "I" style; note the tall vertical windows, the

narrow clapboards and the lack of detail. David Tintle had been an accomplished cowboy working large cattle round-ups. In August of 1890, a horrible accident occurred for the young family when David rolled a wagon loaded with posts over his son's neck, accidentally killing the boy as he rested against the wagon's wheel. *Courtesy Larkspur Historical Society.*

A Barn Raising (Circa 1895-1900). The area between East Cherry Creek and West Cherry Creek, known as Cherry Valley is where the Alderman family settled in the early 1870s. This barn housed full-blooded Jersey and Angus cattle and draft horses. At the time this barn was built, the structure was considered the best in the area. Newton Alderman sits in front, Frank Clingman and Jay Alderman stand on the barn roof; the other man is unknown. *2000.19.5 Courtesy Douglas County History Research Center, Douglas County Libraries.*

Back to Basics (1901). Here young Lawrence Tintle, a member of the East Cherry School student body, holds the bridle of a donkey that may have transported him or one of his brothers to school. Most children walked to school, but some traveled by wagon or horse. This structure is a one-room schoolhouse as were many of the time. A pot-bellied stove was used to heat the schoolroom in winter.

The bathroom facilities were outside and a cool drink of water could be obtained from the hand-pump at the school well. A bucket served as a lunch box with the children eating inside, or outside--weather permitting. The schools often had a barn for the animals as well as a woodshed for fuel to maintain the pot-bellied stove. Not all the students are identified but Lawrence Tintle's brothers, Jay and Frank, are pictured here. Some of the other students, standing in front of the building, are Jay Alderman, Minnie Williams, Lena Aulsebrook, and Frances Williams. *Courtesy Larkspur Historical Society, Wallace Turner Family.*

Let it Snow (Circa 1933). The Blizzard of 1913 put many area residents at risk, cutting them off from civilization for a week with snow depths of about 10 feet. These assaults of nature were not unusual for the pioneers or for the people in this blizzard photograph. Pictured in a four-wheel-drive truck are Melvin Anderson (left) Ralph Wolff (middle) and an unidentified companion (right). Another significant snowfall occurred in the winter of 1946 where once again the winter wonderland took over. *Courtesy Larkspur Historical Society.*

One Hundred-Seventeen Year Old Home (1930). These lovely ladies are (L to R): Evelyn Anglemyer Anderson, Mary Anderson Maas, Aleen Maas and Norma Sampson standing in front of a home that was at the time owned by rancher Wenzel Jaksch. David Meyer, a homesteader, who came to the Lake Gulch area in 1878, started this ranch. This home, built in 1887, is made of Rhyolite and is still standing near Upper Lake Gulch Road. Norma Sampson was a teacher and spent her first year teaching at the red brick schoolhouse, also on this property, called the Upper Lake Gulch School. *Courtesy Ginny Suelzle.*

In Home Business (Circa 1900). William and Flora (Whittier) Wheeler with sons, Forrest and Emerald, and Hattie Whittier stand outside the Case Post Office where Hattie was postmistress, this was also the Whittier home. The Whittiers had owned this land since 1881, when the area was

known as Rock Ridge. The Case Post Office was named after John A. Case. In 1913, the name was again changed, to Irving, in honor of Washington Irving Whittier. Whittier, a man of many talents, had been a teacher, minister, editor, publisher, civil war veteran, and dairyman. *654.13 Courtesy Douglas County History Research Center, Douglas County Libraries.*

Community Spirit (Circa 1900). The Case Grange building in the Cherry Valley area was once owned by the Whittier family. Granges served as agricultural community centers and were built and paid for by the people of the grange. Ranchers joined the Grange for such amenities as parties, meetings and community problem-solving. The organization of the Grange Movement in 1867 provided farmers across the country with a vehicle for having their issues heard in Washington D. C. *654.10 Courtesy Douglas County History Research Center, Douglas County Libraries.*

Chapter Four

Highlands Ranch and Daniels Park

Reinventing Itself

by
The Castle Rock Writers

The Beginning of a Legacy. (Circa 1920). From approximately 1890 to 1901, John W. Springer acquired land and property that he continued to expand upon for almost 30 years. He called the property the John W. Springer Cross Country Horse and Cattle Ranch. It is here that he raised his pride and joy, three prizewinning stallions and 150 pure bred Oldenberg mares. This special breed of horse originally came from the Grand Duchy of Oldenberg in Northern Germany and was known for their specific color, weight and height - an average of 16 hands. Springer and his wife Eliza Clifton Hughes, moved from Illinois to Colorado believing the dry climate would improve Eliza's health. Unfortunately, Eliza died in 1904. Five years later, Springer married Isabelle Patterson. He continued to improve on his original home, but now called the mansion Castle Isabelle in honor of his second wife. However, the marriage was doomed and ended in divorce. Isabelle was involved in an embarrassing scandal involving the death of one of her paramours at the Brown Palace Hotel. Springer sold the property to Waite Phillips in the 1920s and married Jeanette Elisabeth Lotave in 1934. He died in 1945 after acquiring more than 23,000 acres of land in and around the area we now call Highlands Ranch. *Courtesy Phil Brook Art Museum. (EW)*

A Mansion on the Prairie. (Circa 1921). From a relatively modest beginning, John W. Springer built his property and land to finally include more than 23,000 acres in northern Douglas County. When the mansion was finished, it comprised 14 bedrooms, 11 bathrooms, multiple fireplaces a billiard room, butler's quarters and much more. During the 1920s Springer's daughter sold the property to Waite Phillips, brother of the Phillips Petroleum magnates. Other owners of the property have been Frank Kistler and Lawrence Phipps, Jr. *Courtesy Phil Brook Art Museum. (EW)*

An Entrepreneur. (Circa 1921). Waite Phillips and his identical twin brother Wiate were born in Iowa in 1883. As many young people did in those times, they left the family farm and traveled west to seek their fortune. Waite eventually became a millionaire through his endeavors in the rich oil fields of Tulsa, Oklahoma. Waite, together with two other brothers, Frank and L.E., became the leading oil producers in Oklahoma. In the 1920s, Waite purchased the mansion and surrounding land, and gave it the name of Highland Ranch. *Courtesy Phil Brook Art Museum. (EW)*

A Shetland Pony in the Family Room. (1923-24). Elliott Phillips is seen sitting on his pony in the family room at the Highlands Ranch mansion. He was barely three years of age when this photograph was taken, so he has no recollection of the actual photograph or the event but Mr. Phillips stated, "…I don't remember much about that time in my life, but I do remember my little pony. I had a photograph taken in the family room…and I also remember that my sister had a little brown mare called Merry-go-round." *Courtesy Phil Brook Art Museum. (EW)*

Pleasant Memories (Circa 1970). A contemporary photograph of the windmill at the Highlands Ranch mansion. Elliott Phillips recalls that as a child, he and his family visited the ranch many times after moving to New Mexico. He said, "I recall that we had a windmill on the ranch and my sister and I used to go up there all the time. In around 1923-24, my father purchased a ranch in New Mexico that he later donated to the Boy Scouts of America. I believe that property was about 97,000 acres. Anyway, after my father bought the ranch in New Mexico, he kind of lost interest in the Highland Ranch property and he sold it. I think it changed hands several times after our family owned it." *Courtesy The Denver Post. (EW)*

63

A Woman's Home is Her Castle (1998). A castle of unusual elegance and beauty sits atop a rocky mesa in northern Douglas County, north of Highway 85 and just west of Daniel's Park Road. The mansion, with its 15th century Scottish architecture, can hold its own against its neighbors in Castle Pines Village, but in 1926 it was a "chin-dropper." The imposing 11,000 square foot structure boasts 24 rooms, eight bedrooms, a great hall with a minstrel loft and winding staircases. There are four towers with gargoyles and a six-stall garage. The outdoor pool has recently been demolished to enlarge the patio. There are spectacular views from any window on any level. A tour of the castle reveals details of construction, glimpses into the lives of its owners, and a close look at the antique furniture, priceless art and rare book collection. In 1996, Tweet Kimball, owner of Cherokee Ranch established a private foundation enabling her to donate her art, furniture, land and cattle operation to the foundation. She also placed a conservation easement on the land thus protecting the area as a wildlife sanctuary. *Courtesy Cherokee Ranch and Castle Foundation. (LA)*

Just a Small Shack Please! (Circa 1933). When Burnham and Merrill Hoyt were approached by Charles Alfred Johnson in 1924, the plan was to design a "thatched-roof cottage" suitable for a hunting lodge. Two years and many design changes later, a castle emerged. "It was the best contract I ever had" quipped Burnham. In 1926, Charles and his wife Alice moved into their new home with their two small boys. They named their castle "Charlford" after the boys. Charles Johnson, who lives in Denver, once remarked, "There were (in 1926) no houses at all between Daniels Park Road and Cherry Hills Village." *Courtesy Cherokee Ranch and Castle Foundation. (LA)*

Now That's a Lot of Bull! (1958). Tweet Kimball bought "Charlford" in 1954 from the Johnson's sons and promptly changed the name to "Cherokee Ranch". She filled the castle with her antique furniture, art collection and rare books. When the wine cellar was properly filled she set about to "stock" her new cattle operation. Much to the dismay of local ranchers, she imported Santa Gertrudis cows and bulls from the King Ranch in Texas. The breed is a cross between Brahma cows and Texas shorthorns. Red in color, these cattle had never been raised in a cold climate before. Tweet's cattle operation flourished and the locals adjusted. Pictured here Tweet is hand feeding her beloved bulls. Notice the "signature" outfit: a dress, jewelry, lipstick and her rubber working boots! *Courtesy Cherokee Ranch and Castle Foundation. (LA)*

© Colorado Historical Society

The Bike Trail (Circa 1904-1909). An unknown man, girl and woman pose for this photograph on the Alameda Bridge over the South Platte River. The woman sports a rifle in contrast to her feminine attire. More than 100 years ago, many people traveled from Denver to Monument on a bicycle path that followed Broadway to the City Ditch where they rode the ditch to Littleton, and on into Douglas County. Then on to the Highline Canal and/or Broadway where they picked up the Denver to Colorado Springs wagon road (presently Highway 85). The route took in the western edge of present day Highlands Ranch where cyclists took refreshments at Dave Cook's Ranch on the east side of Highway 85 north of Sedalia. Since the round trip to Monument was over 100 miles, many people shipped themselves and their bikes by train to Monument and then rode the 52 miles back to Denver. Some believed the return trip was less strenuous because it was "down hill" all the way. *CHS-L2409 Courtesy Colorado Historical Society, Western History Collection.* *(EW)*

Destination Palmer Lake/Monument. (1900). This unknown young woman stands next to her bicycle in Monument wearing a shorter skirt than is normally seen for that period. Women's long skirts often caused problems because they became entangled in the bike's chain mechanism. The solution was simple: make a kind of latticework design across the open chain using narrow gauge wire or string. This enclosed the chain mechanism and enabled the women's skirts to fly out behind them without worry.

The bicycle seen in the photograph is typical of those used in the late 1900s. A Montrose bicycle could be purchased for $16.95 on the low end but a Columbia bicycle could cost upwards of $75-$100. Many women saw their bicycles as a means of freedom where one could meet young men without a chaperon being present. A favorite place to stop was at Perry Park and Palmer Lake areas, Perry Park for its impressive natural rock formations and Palmer Lake for the boating facilities. *Courtesy Lucretia Vaile Museum. (EW)*

The Welte School (1930-1931). In 1899, District 9 recognized the Dry Creek School, later known as the Welte School. Usually there were no more than 10 pupils and most of these were from the Welte Cheese Ranch, also known as the Big Dry Creek farm. The school was located on Daniel's Park Road, one mile south of County Line Road. Frank Renner bought the building after the school closed in 1950 and then moved it to his property. This group is the class of 1930-1931. Pictured (L to R): Grace Dell Bates, Matilda Dietrich, Elizabeth Renner, Florence Carlson (the teacher) and Elwood Jewell. *654.02 Courtesy Douglas County History Research Center, Douglas County Libraries. (KM)*

Immigrant Family Takes Root (Date unknown). Pictured is a cheese wrapper advertising "Welte's Full Cream Cheese." The word "Thoroughbred" can also be seen on the wrapper. In 1879, Johann Welte, his wife Theresa and brother-in-law Plaziduo Gassner homesteaded in north central Douglas County. They purchased land for $700 and began a dairy farm that consisted 21 cows. Soon the dairy was producing a brick cheese and their signature Limburger Cheese, given the name after the Limburg Province in Belgium where it was first sold. *Courtesy Douglas County History Research Center, Douglas County Libraries. (EW)*

PHILIP RENNER

Big Dry Creek Cheese Ranch
Manufacturer of Welte's Full Cream Cheese
Phone Littleton 763
P. O. Box 25
LITTLETON, COLORADO

Flooded Schoolhouse (1924). Plum Creek Elementary School in northwestern Douglas County was demolished before the Chatfield Dam was finished; the area is now under the waters of Chatfield Reservoir. The students were taught the basics; reading, writing and arithmetic, but also courses in geography, grammar, language, United States history and physiology. The teachers also monitored students for the interest they took in classes, work habits, citizenship and the overall health of the pupil. One room of the school was for grades one through four, and the larger of the two classrooms was for the students of the fifth through eighth grades. *Courtesy Marlene Thomas. (SK)*

The Ladies Rule at School (1924). (L to R): Mrs. Anna Bean, one of two teachers pictured here at the Plum Creek Elementary School, taught first through fourth grades in what was called the school's "Little Room." Mrs. Bennett, Douglas County Schools Superintendent stands next to Mrs. Serena Barr, also a teacher at the Plum Creek School. She taught fifth through eighth grades in what was referred to as the school's "Big Room". It was said that Mrs. Barr helped to change students' lives by providing a "hot lunch" before there was a hot lunch program, and helping her students in any way she could. *Courtesy Marlene Thomas. (SK)*

The Governor's Home (June 15, 1930). Elias M. Ammons became Governor of Colorado and served from 1913-1915; he also served in the State Legislature and was elected State Senator. Ammons was part of a movement to start a state park system in Colorado, so it may be appropriate that the home he built and lived in is now under the Chatfield Reservoir and part of the Chatfield State Park. This area is the very northwestern part of Douglas County. The Cornell family later occupied the home before it became part of the state park system. *Courtesy Marlene Thomas.* (SK)

A Man of Many Titles (Date unknown). The Honorable Rufus Clark was also known as "Dad Clark", "Potato Clark" and the "Potato King of Colorado". He made a great deal of money from his large land holdings, some of which were situated on what is now the Highlands Ranch Golf Club. He grew and harvested potatoes and other vegetables that he sold to prospectors in the area during the gold rush. Philanthropic and civic-minded Mr. Clark donated land and money locally as well as a donation from the sale of potatoes to the victims of the great Chicago fire in 1871. *Courtesy F-18726 Denver Public Library. (SK)*

PRETTY WOMAN RANCH – DOUGLAS CO.
STAGE STOP – CIRCA – 1862.

SKETCH FROM PAINTING

Known as a Beauty (Date unknown). It was said that Elizabeth Richardson was not only an extraordinarily beautiful woman, but also an astute businesswoman. In 1861, Elizabeth and her husband, Sylvester, settled in Douglas County on the Plum Creek Divide. The land was soon to be known as The Pretty Woman Ranch. The ranch was located on a stage route along the First Territorial Road and became a favorite place for travelers to stop for refreshments and supplies. However, in 1864, political maneuverings and alleged favoritism among local big wigs altered the Territorial Road's route. This meant that instead of taking travelers to the Richardson's Ranch, where it is said they enjoyed the hospitality (and the beauty) of Elizabeth, they now bypassed the Richardson's ranch altogether. Unhappy with the turn of events, Richardson lost interest in his ranch and sold it to George Riley in 1868. However, a gentleman never forgets a beauty, and one man remembers that he saw Mrs. Richardson many years later and she was still a very attractive woman. *Courtesy Ann D. Zugelder's estate. (EW)*

Hunting Coyotes (Circa 1930). Lawrence Phipps, Jr. started the tradition of the Arapahoe Hunt at the Phipps Highland Ranch in 1929. The ranch was located east of Louviers, with a commanding view of the Front Range. Hunt Master, Lawrence Phipps III, carried on the hunt tradition. Unlike east coast and English fox hunting, the Arapahoe Hunt pursued coyotes. The purpose was the chase, not to slay a coyote, which meant a fun cross-country ride on horseback. The horses were bred and schooled at the ranch, where they started hunting at the age of five years and hunted up to their early 20s. The average hunt was 25 miles long and the ranch boasted 168 jumps. The Colorado's cold, dry climate can cause a scent to be lost in five minutes, giving the edge always to the coyote. Coyotes chased on horseback were recorded as early as 1900, when the *Denver Times* wrote an article about a meet in Byers. An article ran in December 1902, featured women riding sidesaddle to a coyote hunt on Wild Cat Mountain. George Beeman, Master of the Hounds, is seen here, ready for the hunt at Highlands Ranch. *Courtesy Louise Beeman Hier. (KM)*

The Chase Is On (Circa 1930). A huntsman knows his purebred English foxhounds by their particular sound. When the hounds pick up a scent they give off a soulful howl, which is described as "giving tongue." Hounds, (not "dogs",) come in a combination of shades: brown, white, tan and black; they begin their training for the hunt at six months. The ranch raised 79 hounds at a time. The hounds were paired as "couples" making the number of couples 39 and one half, of which one third would be dispatched for the hunt. Pictured here are George Beeman and daughter, Barbara. *Courtesy Louise Beeman Hier. (KM)*

Tally-Ho (Circa 1930). Pictured here is George Beeman, whose family homesteaded in Douglas County in 1876. He became the huntsman for the Arapahoe Hunt in the late 1920s for the Phipps Highland Ranch. His job was to manage the hounds and horses. As huntsman, Beeman would shout "tally-ho," signaling to the field of riders the hounds had picked up the coyote scent. His riding attire consisted of a scarlet coat, breeches, white cravat, black velvet cap and black hunt boots. Beeman's association with the hunt lasted 62 years. *Courtesy Louise Beeman Hier. (KM)*

Dinky Rides Again (Circa 1920). Tom Davis was hired as caretaker of an area of the ranch owned by Miss. Florence Martin, a wealthy woman from Denver. According to a local newspaper, Miss Martin purchased "Section thirty-one, a part of the Failing Ranch, lying about two and one-half miles east of Louviers, and will commence the erection of a magnificent $100,000 summer home thereon in the near future..." but planning permission hit a snag and so Miss Martin gifted the 1,000 acre site to City of Denver as a philanthropic gesture.

Mr. Davis is seen here surveying the area on his favorite horse Dinky as he poses for a photograph in front of the shelter at Daniel's Park. Vintage motorcars can be seen parked to the side of the shelter as a man looks out over the park. Louise Beeman Hier, Tom Davis's granddaughter remembers the duties of her grandfather, "...he worked as a caretaker/ranger for Miss Martin and made sure trash was removed, etc. He also kept a lookout for gypsies in the area. They used to come by every so often—we don't know where they came from, or where they went to, but I remember them clearly." *Courtesy Mrs. Louise Beeman Hier. (EW)*

74

Riding the Homestead (Circa 1920). Many people took advantage of the Homestead Act, signed into law by President Lincoln May 20, 1862. This act allowed individuals to acquire 160 acre parcels of land, provided they lived on the land for 5 years. However, after six months, the homesteader could purchase the land for $1.25 per acre. Tom Davis homesteaded the area around Daniel's Park in 1895 with his wife and their seven children. Here Tom enjoys a large cigar as he and his horse Dinky look over the area, which is roughly where Castle Pines North is located today. *Courtesy Mrs. Louise Hier. (EW)*

Cheers! (Circa 1900). Tom Davis raises what looks like a glass of beer as if in celebration to the person taking the photograph. He wears bib overalls with the pant legs folded up to suit his short stature. He sports a thick moustache; a hat perched on the back of his head as he smokes a corncob pipe. Of Irish heritage, he was known to dance an Irish jig and even teased his family that he could do so at the ripe old age of 84 years. Note his home is set upon a stone base; the clapboard finish is typical of homes built in the era. *Courtesy Mrs. Louise Hier. (EW)*

A Picnic in Daniel's Park. (Circa 1920-30). Many people traveled from Denver to Daniel's Park to enjoy a day out of the hustle and bustle of the city. Although the people in this photograph are not identified, the natural rock formations in the park are easily identified and have changed little to this day. Note the vintage cars on the bluff, and a horse is clearly seen behind the third tree in the center of the photograph. The men wear nice suits, shirts and hats. The women wear "flapper" type hats and their clothes reflect a period in or around 1920-1930. *Courtesy Mrs. Louise Hier. (EW)*

Not a Sidewinder (Circa 1920-1939). John Oben, Tom Davis's nephew, liked to hunt rattlesnakes at Daniel's Park. Louise Hier recalls, "…the snake in this photograph is not a sidewinder but a regular rattlesnake that were prolific in the area." Mrs. Hier remembers that visitors to their home often hunted rattlesnakes to keep the numbers down because "…rattlers not only harm people, but they bite the horses too, so it's best to keep the numbers down. The best catch would be a nest, where all the baby rattlers could be caught in one go–that kept them under control." *Courtesy Mrs. Louise Hier. (EW)*

Chapter Five

Larkspur and Perry Park

A Place to Settle and Play

by
Susan Koller

Larkspur - Col.

The More Things Change the More They Stay the Same (1910). A well-known feature of the Larkspur landscape is Monkey Face on the east side of Raspberry Butte. It is one of the most distinguishable landmarks in the county. In 1910, when this photo was taken, the population of Larkspur was 201. The 2000 census stated the population to be just 234, an increase of only 33 people.

Time may pass in Larkspur, but how much has really changed? Early on, timber cut from the hillsides all around Larkspur and Perry Park provided wood for building the town, the railroads, and the ranches. Cattle for meat and dairy products built up the economy. The area also developed as a resort spot. Larkspur and Perry Park were just far enough from Denver to become a "get-away" from the hustle and bustle of Denver and the brown cloud that was present even in the late 1800s. The brown cloud could be viewed from a high point in Perry Park. Today, as in 1910, trees abound, cattle roam the hills, trains pass through daily, and people still flock to the area to live or for relaxation and pleasure. *Courtesy Maureen Wysocki.*

Still Standing (Circa 1914). This photo offers a taste of what Larkspur looked like before the flood of 1965. The large white building at left of photograph is the Carlson & Frink Creamery. At the height of production, 800 lbs of milk flowed through the creamery daily. The blacksmith's shop was located across the street and adjacent was a mercantile store. At the end of the road, center back of photograph is the Larkspur Schoolhouse. The railroads carried passengers and area products such as gypsum, clay, lumber, dairy products and cattle. The area once boasted two sawmills, a hardware store and the Victoria Casino, among other buildings. *Courtesy American Federation of Human Rights, Co-Masonry.*

Cream of the Dairy Industry (Circa 1920). Interior of the Carlson Frink Creamery branch in Sedalia depicts a typical creamery of the era. The Carlson Frink Creamery, based in Larkspur, quickly spread to other areas, such as Sedalia, but also expanded outside the county. Quality products, such as the famous Black Canyon Cheese and the trustworthiness of a good businessman made Mr. Frink's opinion much sought after. The Record Journal advertisements in 1919 and 1920 showed that Mr. Frink was a conscientious businessman who cared about the dairy farmers. *687.591 Courtesy Douglas County History Research Center, Douglas County Libraries.*

Cyclone at Larkspur (Circa 1900). The Larkspur Schoolhouse was erected in 1884 on what is now the Fox Farm Ranch Road area. The building was moved using log skids in 1890 to the northeast area of the Village of Larkspur. What was described as a cyclone destroyed the schoolhouse on August 3rd 1912. The Record Journal's story also reported; "The funnel-shaped cloud dropped to the earth near the schoolhouse narrowly missing the Santa Fe depot and section house." The students above enjoyed a one room schoolhouse; their teacher probably boarded with the family of one of her students, the tradition of the times. *Courtesy Betty Prince.*

The World at Larkspur's Doorstep (Circa 1918). The Denver and Rio Grande Railroad and the Atchison, Topeka and Santa Fe Railway were a large part of life in Larkspur and because of them the world could travel to the area. People came to attend meetings held on the American Federation of Human Rights grounds and noticed the resort-like feeling that the area had; its fresh air, open spaces, views, peace and quiet and wild life. The Denver & Rio Grande Depot in Larkspur is the building in the middle; this was the first of two depots for the small but active area. *Courtesy American Federation of Human Rights, Co-Masonry.*

An Important Resource
(Circa 1900). Since 1858
logging in Douglas
County was a strong
industry. Many
sawmills were built,
including the D.C.
Oakes mill in 1859 at the
base of Hunt Mountain.
Log homes were built
with the trees found on
the property by pioneers
and homesteaders. Rich
with pine trees,
Larkspur was an
important railroad stop
for timber. In the 1920s,

logging declined and the main industry for the area became dairying. The lumber camp
that adjoined the town of Larkspur along with the sawmills disappeared. Cliff McClure is
pictured here in the Jackson Creek area logging and hauling wood. *Courtesy Larkspur
Historical Society.*

Pioneer Families Band Together (Date unknown). A hearty pioneering family in Douglas
County, Benjamin and Mary Quick lived close to Perry Park. Benjamin settled in the area
early in 1861. In 1868, he and other settlers built Fort Washington around the Quick's early
home, for safety from frequent and surprise Indian raids. This fort covered more than an
acre and included a well. The Quick's home, listed with the National Register of Historic
Places, is built of Rhyolite and stands close to Perry Park Road. The drawing of Mary was
taken from a photo of her dated November 19, 1889. *Courtesy Dottie Mullis.*

Room for Two Spares (Circa 1900). Notice the extra wheels in the bed of Mr. McClure's mail wagon; he was determined that a broken wheel would not keep the mail from being delivered. Now imagine living in the early 1900s. Your ranch has no phone or radio and the post office is a day's ride away. Mr. McClure's mail wagon would then be a great convenience, saving time and effort by bringing the outside world to the ranch. Home delivery of mail helped to improve conditions of many of the country's roads, because the road conditions determined delivery service. *Courtesy Larkspur Historical Society.*

Large Families a Necessity (Circa 1889). The Nickson Family gathered for a photograph on the porch of their home. Mr. George Nickson is seated with Sarah on his knee, next to him is Mrs. Sarah Nickson with their youngest Charles on her lap. The other children from bottom are (L to R): Mary, Andrew, Joseph, Elizabeth, Annie and George Jr. The family's lives in the county started on West Plum Creek, north of the present Perry Park, about 1872, in a log cabin built from the trees on their land. Native Americans were common visitors to the ranch, camping in Perry Park. *Courtesy Dottie Mullis.*

Fresh Air Beckons (Circa 1923) "Be free thinkers, be aware and be service focused." This was and is the philosophy of the American Federation of Human Rights. Six hundred acres were purchased in 1912 in Larkspur for the members. Some were Pennsylvania miners with respiratory problems, sent to convalesce in Colorado's dry recuperative climate. In 1915, the members built their headquarters, shown here, with bricks they made by hand. Chosen partially for access to transportation, the building was built close to the Atchison, Topeka and Santa Fe Depot. A well was dug and the water was offered to the community for $1 per month. *Courtesy American Federation of Human Rights, Co-Masonry.*

A Fall Wedding (October 10, 1905). This photo was taken on the day Mr. I.J. Noe and Miss. Claudie E. Wilson were united in marriage. Named for his Uncle Isaac Jegirtha Noe, this I.J. was called "Junior." Early in their marriage, they lived with his father's family (Jerre Noe) helping out on the ranch. Junior was the eldest of eight children; born in 1884, attended the Larkspur school, was caretaker at the American Federation of Human Rights grounds in Larkspur, and also lived in Greenland and Castle Rock. Claudie was I.J.'s first wife - she died in 1925. *Courtesy Noe Family.*

Packing a Colt (Circa 1905). The Lamb family posed at home on their 720 acre Lamb Ranch near Larkspur. Front row (L to R): Jennie, Gertrude, Fred, Mr. Carr Lamb, and Mrs. Ann Lamb Back row (L to R): Hildred, Grace and Helen. The hard-working ranch family had the L/L brand on their dairy herd. Mr. Lamb supplemented the family's income working as a county commissioner. He was said to carry a "Colt 38" to protect against cattle rustlers. Hildred washed the milk cans that went to the creamery, earning one cent a can. *Courtesy Betty Prince.*

Making Hay (Circa 1916). At about the time of this photo, hay was one of America's biggest products. Alfalfa and clover were typical crops grown for stock feed to make hay. Everyone chipped in at haying time as time and good weather were of the essence. Drying the hay was an important task and wet or over-dried hay could affect its nutritional value. The children working this field are Clara, Kenneth, and Clifford McClure. *Courtesy Larkspur Historical Society, Wallace Turner Family.*

A Trip to Market (Circa 1920). The Saare grocery, located at the intersection of Frink and County Roads, is partially shown here with unidentified gentlemen. The two men on the right probably worked at the store; notice the sleeve protectors they have on their arms. Another grocery store in the Larkspur area was called Pearmans. In September of 1943, they placed an ad in the Record Journal saying they had purchased all the peaches of a Palisade Colorado peach-grower for their customers' advantage. Pearmans again advertised on April 14, 1944: "Custom hatching, offering hen, turkey, duck and geese eggs." *Courtesy Larkspur Historical Society, Wallace Turner Family.*

A Child's Model (Circa 1944-45). This photograph of the Allen Grocery store shows Norma Jean Allen leaving, holding a sucker and two other small bags clutched in her hand, possibly filled with candy. The ads on the door, around and in the window are all for tobacco. The MODEL poster in the window describes a 1943 promotion offering people the chance to vote for their favorite model from a selection of models featured in on-going advertisements. *Courtesy Larkspur Historical Society, Wallace Turner Family.*

Rampart Range Beckons (Circa 1900). The wide expanse of over 500 acres shows the Upper T Ranch, the Rampart Range and Pike National Forest to the west (background). Upton Treat Smith, a pioneer of Douglas County, homesteaded the area in 1869; this would become his dairy ranch. Note the many haystacks. Feed for the dairy herd, they almost take over the ranch in their size and take on the look of buildings. Mr. Smith's four children--Hattie, Edwin, Guy and Roger--were born in Douglas County and his family stayed in the area for 50 years. *Courtesy Larkspur Historical Society.*

A Round of Golf, Rocky Mountain Style (Circa 1900). This manor house built in 1891, (although with some additions and modernization), is the Perry Park Country Club. It originally served as the home of Charles A. Roberts, secretary of the Redstone Town, Land and Mining Company, which bought 3,980 acres from landowner John Perry in 1888. A resort area was planned and Mr. Perry became a principal stockholder in the company. The area was developed and plans were drawn up for other buildings. Frederick Law Olmsted was hired to help turn this Colorado property into a beautifully landscaped desirable destination. *Courtesy Perry Park Country Club.*

85

Thanksgiving Turkey (July 9, 1947). You may recognize Hunt Mountain and Larkspur Butte in this photograph's background. B.J. Bussing and John Hammond are pictured here among the April hatched broad breasted bronze turkeys, a flock that numbered 4,000. The land pictured here holds the ruins of William Crull's 1874 homestead cabin. The logs from the cabin have been time dated to 1865. Crull's ranch was just north of the settlement of Huntsville. *Courtesy Larkspur Historical Society, Bonnie (Hammond) Bell.*

Indian Namesake (1901). Nanichant Inn was a Perry Park establishment built about 1889 and destroyed by fire in the 1920s. After first opening for business, it changed names many times: Hotel Echo, Clifton Inn, Narrichant Inn and Nanichant Hotel. The Inn was named for the 300 feet high Nanichant Rock that stands close by, the name being derived from the Indian pronunciation "nar-ee-charnt", which translated means Echo. Perry Park was a favorite place to visit especially when the fancy Concord stage brought patrons to this resort hotel. X-21223 *Courtesy Denver Public Library.*

A Very Dashing Couple (Circa 1918). They may look the part, but thoughts of Bonnie and Clyde couldn't be further from the truth for John Hammond and his future wife Minnie May Phillips. This couple is lovingly posed in front of his first car, a Model T Ford Roadster. They were married in 1924 and shared a lifetime together. Mr. Hammond worked at many pursuits in Douglas County; these included the office of Deputy Sheriff before being elected Sheriff in 1947 and serving for 24 years. John Hammond also owned the Larkspur Garage for a time and a ranch in the Larkspur area. Minnie was also very accomplished, fun loving and cared for her family deeply. Minnie kept the books for all of her husband's businesses, which included the garage and the ranch mentioned above. She was a basketball star at the high school in Elizabeth where the happy couple first met. John and Minnie Hammond were united in marriage for 54 years and had three daughters. *Courtesy Larkspur Historical Society, Bonnie (Hammond) Bell, special thanks to Beryl (Hammond) Livingood.*

Hunting Trip
(Circa 1909). Hunting for sport and camping in Colorado are Douglas County native Edwin Smith and his wife Zelma. The Record Journal of August 1928 printed an article entitled "Timely Hints for Camping Trips" Some money-saving suggestions were: a sleeping bag could be fashioned by pinning two  woolen army blankets together, or bedding could be made with newspapers as a good substitute. To make camp shoes wear longer, put heavy glue on the soles and then cover the glue with sawdust. *92001.002.142 Courtesy Douglas County History Research Center, Douglas County Libraries.*

Black Bear Feast (Circa 1940). Douglas County was once described as a "Hunters Paradise." Hunting for survival had pioneers creating interesting recipes such as the ones in the cookbook "Pioneer Potluck." Assembled by volunteers of the State Historical Society of Colorado, it contains recipes for beaver tail, directions for pickling beaver tail and other flavorful ideas. Recipes that used black bear grease in foods, oil, leather and for making soap were readily available. Cliff McClure is pictured with his hunting trophies; he was born in the area and attended the Lone Tree School just north of Perry Park. *Courtesy Larkspur Historical Society, Wallace Turner Family.*

When They Were Called Service Stations (1935). Since first built, the Larkspur Garage was a busy establishment. Situated on Spruce Mountain Road south of Perry Park Avenue, the garage provided gas, tires and

other services for the motorist. In 1918, the owners were Shelton & Shelton and later Hugh Buckner owned the garage. John Hammond worked for Buckner at the time of this photograph and leased the business in the late 30s. *Courtesy Larkspur Historical Society, Bonnie (Hammond) Bell.*

Break-Neck Speed (1936). The Larkspur Garage's tow truck was put to use many times in 1936, and for many years after. The local legend of the area was that brake failure was commonplace for the cars of the time coming down the hill into town. This garage also became a community gathering place as one old-timer remembers going to the garage to box and wrestle with his friend John Hammond. *Courtesy Larkspur Historical Society, Bonnie (Hammond) Bell. Special thanks to Mr. Frank Garcilaso.*

A Change of Seasons (1940). Near Metz Canyon west of Larkspur this ranch is known as the "Ware Place," situated at the beginning of Valley Park south of Perry Park. Nine children were born to Felix and Louisia (Sedbrook) Metz. Felix was a professional rock layer but made a living in Larkspur doing odd jobs. Metz Canyon was named for the Metz family; pioneer families have had many places in the county named for them. Hunt Mountain and Huntsville, three miles north of Larkspur, were named for ranch owner and Territorial Governor, Alexander Cameron Hunt (1867-1869). John D. Perry purchased the area known as Pleasant Park, later named Perry Park. Dawson Butte is named for homesteader Thomas Dawson. Other names like Jackson, Dakan, and Noe are also names of pioneering families; these names can be seen around the area. *Courtesy Larkspur Historical Society, Wallace Turner Family.*

A Bear Hunt (Circa 1946). Larkspur Stockyard is the setting for this photo of Mr. Grover Reed (left) and Mr. Frank Garcilaso (right), pictured with the bear that Frank and his brother Tom had killed the night before the photo was taken. The girls at the far right in the photo are Mr. Garcilaso's sisters. Both of these gentlemen worked for the Denver & Rio Grande Railroad; Mr. Garcilaso worked as a section foreman for 43 years and Mr. Reed was the Depot Agent also serving as postmaster for the railroad. *Courtesy Larkspur Historical Society, Wallace Turner Family. Special thanks to Mr. Frank Garcilaso.*

Best Burgers in Town (1947). The sign reads "Larkspur Café" and has also seen signs reading; "Dew Drop Inn", "Spur" and today "Spur of the Moment." The building was actually built in 1923 as a private home, over 20 years before this photograph was taken. It was moved toward the road and slightly north when it became a cafe, serving burgers and beer and had according to a newspaper ad, "Specials on Sunday," when Mr. and Mrs. C.H. Osten and Son were the proprietors. Worthing Taylor can be seen working on the roof. *Courtesy Larkspur Historical Society.*

Swept Away in The Flood (Circa 1950). This chapel was destroyed in the horrible flood of 1965; the Larkspur Fire Department's new buildings now sit on this land where the Larkspur Chapel once stood. Besides being a place for the community to come together to worship, the community's

children were also taught Sunday school lessons here and the Extension Club, "Friendly Larks", which organized in 1937, held their meetings here also. The building had been turned over to them for their use in the early 1950s. *Courtesy Larkspur Historical Society.*

Renaissance Women *(1950).* Well before the Extension Homemakers Club called "Friendly Larks Club" posed for this picture, groups like these lovely ladies of the Larkspur area held monthly meetings. Their concerns went beyond sewing and canning to include informative talks from local doctors and other health professionals on various health-related subjects. They also featured talks on new products to help the homemaker, modern business methods, fire prevention, gardening, and other subjects to help themselves as well as their community. This photo was taken in front of the Pearmans store in Larkspur. *Courtesy Larkspur Historical Society.*

Chapter Six

Lone Tree

From One Small Tree

by
Kathleen McCoy

A Real Cowboy (Circa 1910). Cowboys have always worn functional outfits, as seen in this picture. The flat brimmed hat was not only worn to shield them from the weather, but could be used to water and feed his horse. The bandana was also a protection against the elements and could be used to hobble (hinder a horse by tying its legs together). It is believed Martha Washington created the first bandana for the American troops, during the Revolutionary War. Chaps is a shortened word for chaparreras, which is like a full length apron split and tied at the waist and knees. Chaps protect the pants from being torn up and are designed so the saddle can be felt between the legs. Two months pay could be invested in the boots alone. The narrow toe of the boot slips easily into the stirrup, while the high heel catches on the stirrup to keep the foot from slipping through, thereby lessening the chance of the foot being caught. Cowboys at the time of this photo frequently carried a Winchester rifle and a Colt six shooter pistol. According to Jonathan Schweiger, a descendent of the John Schweiger family, the subjects pictured are possibly Lester Tuggle and wife, Rose Schweiger. *2004.023.003.001 Courtesy Douglas County History Research Center, Douglas County Libraries.*

Roping Skills (Date unknown). This cowboy is demonstrating his lassoing skills, which evolved from Spanish cowboys, or "vaqueros." In the open range, they would throw a rope over the cattle's horns, throwing it to the ground for sport. Cowboys learned from the vaqueros to braid horsehair or rawhide for lariats, lead ropes, halters and bridles, until fiber rope was introduced from foreign ships in the 1850s. In the early 1900s, gauntlets with cuffs were being worn to protect from rope burns. On the ranch, children would start practicing roping by lassoing cats and ducks. *2004.023.004.001 Courtesy Douglas County Research Center, Douglas County Libraries.*

Wild Horses (Date unknown). This cowboy, who has not lost his hat yet, is "busting a bronco." Once a horse was trained to be ridden, a cowboy might have several to choose from, depending on the job. A "roper" was good for riding while lassoing cattle, a "cutting" horse for separating out cattle, a "swimmer" had a round belly for crossing a river, and a "night" horse avoided prairie dog holes in the dark. The earliest known rodeo, where bronco riding was an event, was held at Deer Trail, Colorado on July 4, 1869. *2004.023.004.002 Courtesy Douglas County Research Center, Douglas County Libraries.*

An Explosive Skirt (Circa 1916). This is a 1916 Model T Ford touring car. If this group is preparing for a country outing, that might account for the woman's shorter skirt. Women cut off the length of the skirt for easier walking and sometimes sewed buckshot in the hem to keep the skirt from billowing out in the wind. The woman holding the baby is thought to be Ruth Schweiger, wife of George Schweiger with her son, John G. Schweiger, born December 16, 1915. *2004.023.006.001 Courtesy Douglas County Research Center, Douglas County Libraries.*

From a Single Tree (Circa 1916). Jonathan Schweiger said the three brothers drew straws to see who should get married. His great uncle John consequently wedded Anna Scheider. Their western style Victorian farmhouse was built between 1894-1910, a lone tree stood in the front yard. Jack O'Boyle, Mayor of Lone Tree explains, "The Lone Tree builder called it that for no particular tree. We couldn't find the tree from which all us nuts fell; in 1998 on Arbor Day, we planted a Colorado blue spruce on the corner of Lincoln Parkway and Yosemite and named it Lone Tree!" *2004.023.002.002 Courtesy Douglas County History Research Center, Douglas County Libraries.*

Music in the Canyon (1934). "Happy Canyon" was named by John Schweiger after a singing cowboy named "Happy" Jack Johnson. Jack would ride his horse throughout the canyon, filling it with his beautiful voice. It reminded John of the singing he used to hear in the Tyrolean Mountains of Austria. This happy group on the front porch of the Schweiger family house should probably be taken seriously, as they are sporting 5 guns! Note that the smiling woman in the polka dot dress is within easy reach of the rifle behind her. *2004.023.006.002 Courtesy Douglas County Research Center. Douglas County Libraries.*

An Area School (Circa 1890-1900). John Schweiger donated land for the Happy Canyon School, located today east of I-25 at Surrey Ridge Road. The school opened in the 1880s. Prior to that, a cabin on the ranch was used as a classroom when cowboys were not occupying it as a bunkhouse. The area was designated District Twenty-eight and the teacher was paid twenty-five dollars a month. The schoolhouse was built for the children in the area. John and Anna's seven children: Rose, Anna, John Jr., Max, George, Joseph and Pauline, also attended there. *2004.023.001.002 Courtesy Douglas County Research Center, Douglas County Libraries.*

First Family (Date unknown). When one reflects on Lone Tree's settlement, the family name Schweiger transcends all others. The three brothers, John, Joseph, Jacob and their parents migrated from Austria in 1866. In 1872, they were among the first permanent settlers in the north central part of the county, ranching in a canyon east of Daniels Park and continuing northeast toward Surrey Ridge. The Schweiger's Happy Canyon Ranch was established within today's Ridge Gate development in the city of Lone Tree. Jonathan Schweiger, who is the great, great nephew of the pioneer brothers' father said, the Schweiger brand was originally recorded in 1897. The brand was transferred in Douglas County to John's son in 1913. Jonathan said the brand is now in his name and is registered in Logan/Morgan County. A brand is identification for cattle, horses, mules, sheep, goats and asses. He confirmed the following: violating the law that protects a branded animal, whether it is theft, selling or killing is a class 6 felony, punishable by imprisonment in the state penitentiary and a fine. He should know; Jonathan Schweiger is a Brand Inspector for the State of Colorado. *93005-043-2 Courtesy Douglas County History Research Center, Douglas County Libraries.*

Water as Valuable as Gold (Circa 1910-1915). From 1899 until 1919, Colorado ranked the highest in the nation for irrigating its farm land. The Schweigers, however, used a technique called dry land farming, which relied on the moisture from winter and spring snow melts to sprout the seeds planted the previous fall. For the house, they did have a cistern, (a large tank for holding water). A pump, driven by a windmill, was used to fill the cistern. They raised cattle, wheat, oats, alfalfa hay and corn. This photo was taken in the southeastern part of the county at the Bartruff-Bihlmeyer Ranch, but it shows corn being harvested by a two-horse team, which could work about 4 acres a day. The Schweiger Ranch would have harvested corn with this method. During the early years on the ranch land prices ranged from $2.50 to $6.00 an acre. Corn was especially important to a ranch using both horsepower and cattle production, because corn and dry corn fodder were often used to feed these livestock. With a spring planting schedule, folklore advises corn should be planted when the oak leaves are about the size of a squirrel's ear. In Douglas County, that would be the native scrub oak leaf bush. *93005 Courtesy Douglas County History Research Center, Douglas County Libraries.*

The History Lives On (2004). On September 16, 2004, the Schweiger family attended a ceremony designating their Happy Canyon Ranch as a Douglas County Historic Landmark. The city of Lone Tree, in cooperation with Coventry Development Corporation, worked to secure grant money from the Colorado State Historic Fund for a Historic Structure Assessment. This will guide a restoration project coming none too soon for the deteriorating buildings, which include house, barn, sheds, brick silo, chicken coop, beekeeper's storeroom and windmill. (Note in this photo of Jonathan Schweiger with grandson, Coy John Waitley, the asphalt shingles that now cover the original clapboard siding on the ranch house are falling off. The porch concrete base is jacked up by a beam, and the porch floor is covered with a plywood board.) Coventry and city council members, who attended the ceremony, have hopes of the property being used as a working farm museum or possibly a non-profit equestrian therapeutic/training site for the disabled, known as the Pegasus Project. *Courtesy Kathy McCoy.*

Gunshot Silo (2004). Silos are used on farms and ranches to store fodder, (ground up corn stalks or hay to feed cattle and horses). This silo on the Schweiger ranch was built in the 1930s and is still functional, even though it contains debris now, and sports a steer's head. The cylindrical shaped construction is 46 feet high and 15 feet in diameter with a loading chute at the top. The outside walls are built of tile blocks set in mortar and have bullet hole damage, possibly from the steer head being used for target practice. *Courtesy Kathy McCoy.*

From Yale to Lone Tree (Date unknown). The horses used on the Schweiger ranch were "grade" animals, meaning of no particular breed, but the riding style and tack, (saddle and bridle), were western. Pictured is Caroline Ball, mother-in-law to George Schweiger and wife of Frank D. Ball. She was born in Wales in 1860, and came to Douglas County with her family when she

was 11 years old. Mr. Ball's tie to Lone Tree was that as a young man he taught at the Happy Canyon School. He was a Yale graduate and was elected superintendent of Douglas County Schools in 1895. *Courtesy Douglas County History Research Center, Douglas County Libraries.*

Chapter Seven

Louviers

From Rolling Hills to Du Pont Company Town

by
Alice Aldridge-Dennis

Early days in the Area (Circa 1945). Families from the British Isles and Europe settled in Douglas County south of Littleton and north of Sedalia, ranching and farming. On the territorial road between Denver and Colorado City, the area was an interesting, convenient place to live. The year 1871 brought the Denver and Rio Grande narrow gauge railroad, which also connected Denver and Colorado Springs. Charles Turner Newmarch and his wife Elizabeth Mary Ann Perry Newmarch acquired their first 160 acres in 1871. Charles, a well-respected dairyman and breeder, and his wife Elizabeth added land to their ranch over the years, eventually having about 530 acres. Their children were born at the home, including George T. Newmarch (1872), Charles James (1869), Ida Mary Ann (1874), and Elizabeth Lillian (1883). George's children, Howard Newmarch (1898), Turner Newmarch (1903), Ethel Newmarch (1904), and Ruth Newmarch (1912) were also born there. When Charles died, his son George ran the ranch. In 1946, when George Newmarch and his wife retired at age 74, they sold the ranch to Mr. and Mrs. Frank Woodhouse. The original home, built in 1873, burned down shortly thereafter. *Courtesy of the Penley Family.*

The Newmarch Family at the Ranch (Circa 1909). George Thomas Newmarch was born and raised in Douglas County. In the front row of this family photo are Ethel and Turner Newmarch. The second row shows Howard Newmarch, Susan Harlin Newmarch (Mom), George Newmarch (Pop), and Elizabeth Mary Ann Perry Newmarch (Grandma Newmarch). The third row shows Mrs. Roberts and her daughter and two unidentified people. The Newmarch family was one of many families who settled land along the Plum Creek Valley. *Courtesy of the Penley Family*

Early Days *(Circa 1915)* In 1906, E.I. Du Pont de Nemours Company representatives from Delaware scouted out a site for a powder plant south of Littleton. Their goal was to supply the west with dynamite. The 1825 acres of slightly hilly land could contain accidental explosions. Nearby Plum Creek provided water for steam generators. The railroad line provided a supply of workers from Denver. The plant site was named "Toluca" the same name as the nearby Denver and Rio Grande Railroad depot. In 1907, Du Pont named its new company town "Louviers." after Louviers in France. *X-12162 Courtesy Colorado Historical Society, Western History Collection.*

The "Flats" (Circa 1915). Early workers for Du Pont's Louviers plant inhabited tents, hillside caves, and board shanties on the west side of Plum Creek. Life was primitive with no running water, no sewage system, and no established streets. By 1907, one-room frame cottages, approximately 386 square feet, were built on top of railroad ties in the flat area that became known as the "flats." In this photograph, residents of Louviers gathered by home #25. Augusta Creede, known as "Duddie," is the one without the hat. She served as long-time Du Pont telephone operator. *94069.01 Douglas County History Research Center, Douglas County Libraries*

The Doctor's Home (Circa 1913*)*. In 1912, Du Pont hired plant doctor Dr. C.E. Dumke on salary. Families also paid $1 per month to support medical services. The photo shows Mrs. Dumke and daughter Ann on their porch at the south end of town. Gene Hughes was the first boy born in Louviers in  May 1913. (His artwork hangs in Bud's Bar in Sedalia.) The first girl, Edna Johnson, was born in June 1913. Mary Lee Rainey, born at home in 1926, was Dr. Dumke's 1,000th delivery. Two years later, her brother was born at the Presbyterian Hospital in Denver. *Douglas County History Research Center, Douglas County Libraries.*

103

The Du Pont Plant Superintendent's House (Circa 1915). Two early houses in the new town were built for the "bosses," on the hill just above the "flats." Later on, four larger homes were built further up the hill on "Capitol Hill" or "Manager's Row," to accommodate the managers' families. After these homes were completed, the two original houses were used for other employee housing. A plant superintendent and family lived in this home, built in 1911. Women in white dresses look on as family and friends take a spin in the open-air automobile. *X-12166 Courtesy Denver Public Library, Western History Collection*

The Hotel (Circa 1920). The 33-room hotel, built in 1912, provided a first-floor post office, store, pool room, dining room, and hotel manager residence. The second floor housed employees and visitors. The hotel was torn down in 1932 or 1933. A boarding house, nicknamed the "flea club" for the few single men who had to do their own laundry, was then created to house them and visiting VIPs from Du Pont in Delaware. The post office and store were eventually moved to the Clubhouse. Frank Clark is the gentleman without a hat. *94069.03 Courtesy Douglas County History Research Center, Douglas County Libraries.*

Denver & Rio Grande Depot Building (Circa 1910). This depot served people who lived in the Louviers and Kelleytown area. The location is near the original stagecoach stop called "Keystone" or "Kelley's Station." As a railroad stop, it was called "Toluca," a word with Spanish and Indian roots. This was also the name of the telephone and telegraph station. After Louviers was established, the station name was changed to Louviers. By 1932 it was called the Louviers Rio Grande Station. Area residents took the train into Littleton for groceries and other goods. *Courtesy Colorado Railroad Museum Collection*

Louviers Village Club (Circa 1917-1918). Social life in Louviers centered around the clubhouse, built in 1917. Early on, men frequented the card room, and the ladies enjoyed the second floor sitting room. Leather-bound first edition books, shelved behind leaded glass doors, made the first library in the county a grand one. The billiards room was displaced by the grocery store, relocated from the hotel. Families remember free, first-run movies on Friday nights in the community hall. Later, the day was Wednesday. Romantic dances and bowling leagues made life fun. The facility houses the oldest bowling alley in the state. *Courtesy of Hagley Museum and Library*

The Pierce Home/The Old Johns' Place (Circa 2000). This log house sits on land that originally belonged to Gilbert H. Pierce, who purchased 80 acres in Section 34 in 1876. Locals remember it as "the Old Johns' Place," due to the longevity of the Johns family who lived here for many years. Albert L. Johns, from Colorado City, lived here by 1899, and he married local Mary Nickson in 1905. Their children were Alberta, Andrew, and Henry. The Johns family farmed the land, receiving a shipment of pigs in 1913. Albert Johns died in 1940; his wife lived another 23 years. Alberta married Tim Lyons, and they stayed on. *Courtesy Sedalia Historic Fire House Museum.*

"Kelleytown" (Circa 2000). In 1869, Jonathan and Ester Kelley homesteaded along the territorial road. Their "Keystone Ranch" became the stagecoach stop and post office, with Jonathan as postmaster. In 1907, their son William C. Kelley legally dedicated streets and alleys to make "Kelleytown." The town was booming with a hotel, store, barbershop, feed store, and about 50 residents. Du Pont built self-sufficient Louviers nearby, curtailing Kelleytown's success. The Olmstead dairy farm, above, was built in 1900 on part of the Kelley property. Bernard Ely purchased the farm in the 40s; it was demolished in 2001. Today "Kelleytown" is mostly residential. *Courtesy Lamar Noble, Louviers Historic Foundation.*

The Alley Gang (Circa 1935). Life in Louviers was wonderful for children, according to those who grew up there. This is one "alley gang" of Coyote Row ("coyote" with two syllables, not three). Ron Rainey and Sterling Rainey, Jr. are seated. Bob Richardson and Mary Lee Rainey

are standing in the back to the left. Others are unidentified. Sterling's family called him "Junior." His mother explained he would be called "Sterling" when he started school, since he was named for his dad. Little Sterling had asked "Why don't they just call me 'Daddy'?" *Courtesy of Mary Lee Rainey Johnston private collection*

Adventure! (Circa 1930). Hooney (George) Livingood and Dean Dale, shown with a string of fish, loved the outdoors. They and pal Ed Rennison once built a swimming hole on Plum Creek by filling gunnysacks with sand and building a dam. When the Du Pont chemist noticed a dry creek bed, the plant manager walked the creek and found boys splashing and hollering. The boys had to dismantle their work. Later, the understanding manager had a worker dig out a pond with a backhoe, which was filled by artesian springs. Many remember fishing and ice skating there. *Courtesy Beryl Hammond Livingood private collection.*

E.I. Du Pont de Nemours & Company—Louviers, Colorado Works (August 31, 1938). The earliest workers at Du Pont came from various places around the United States. In 1906, George Reed was sent from Ashburn, Missouri to start the dynamite plant at Louviers, making his family the first family there. Joseph Jones, hired for 17.5 cent per hour in 1908, commuted by bicycle from Littleton. Edwin Conrad, first child of Charles and Alta (Bean) Conrad, began working at age 14, walking from his family's ranch west of the plant. William Livingood, who was born in Mancato, Kansas, arrived in Louviers in 1909 at the age of 19. Three years later, he left for the Du Pont Plant in Ashburn, Missouri. There, he married Pearl Barker, and they had ten children, including twins who died at birth and Thelma, who died of burn injuries around age four. The Livingoods moved back to Louviers in a 1929 touring car 18 years after Bill had left, bringing along Granny Barker. Pearl Barker Livingood and the children went back to Ashburn in 1933, so their eleventh child would be born in the same place as the others. As adults, the sons all worked for Du Pont, and most of the daughters married men who worked for or retired from Du Pont. Many of the children and grandchildren of this family still live in Louviers.

This 1938 photo shows how many employees earned their livelihood working for Du Pont. In years to follow, a few women begin to appear in the company photographs. They worked in the office, the box factory, or the shell factory. Some were the widows of plant employees. Due to the products made at the plant, employees were not allowed to carry lighters or matches, and they could not smoke except in a smoking hut. If they were caught possessing matches or smoking, they would lose their jobs immediately. Hunting was also not allowed anywhere in Louviers, due to the danger. If an employee quit or was fired, he and his family had to move within a week to free up the employee housing for someone else. The plant smokestack was a landmark that could be seen for miles. *Courtesy Beryl Hammond Livingood private collection.*

Du Pont Explosives (Circa 1950). Du Pont built the Louviers factory to meet regional needs and avoid shipping dynamite all the way from Hannibal, Missouri or San Francisco, California. The growing western region needed explosives for railroad and road construction, mining, and clearing of land. Du Pont also wanted to ship dynamite to other western states and to the Orient. From 1908 until 1971, the Louviers Dynamite Works produced one billion pounds of dynamite. It also had the distinction of being the longest operating Du Pont dynamite factory. The factory made some of the explosives that created Hoover Dam, Pikes Peak Highway, Moffat Tunnel, Blue River Tunnel, and Glen Canyon Dam. Work at the plant was punctual; the whistle blew for starting time, lunchtime, and ending time on the day shift. The company paid well, but the powder line workers often suffered headaches. George Livingood, who drove Du Pont trucks for 17 years, is shown delivering powder to Clovis, New Mexico. Du Pont maintained its own truck line, delivering to Wyoming, Montana, Utah, and Colorado until the mid-1960s. *Courtesy Beryl Hammond Livingood private collection.*

Camp Fire Girls Trip (1947). Louviers Camp Fire Girls spent a day in Denver, learning "civics" and touring the Capitol, the U.S. Mint, and the Civic Center. (L to R): Edith McKenzie, Jackie Hughes, Betty Lee Shea, Jean Edgeler, Mrs. Elinor Cornell Shea (leader), Yvonne Starr, Bunny Larsen, and Marie "Butch" Bolger. Another time, they camped for a week at Deckers, using Joe Jones' cabin. Mrs. Shea, a resident of Louviers for 46 years, loved being leader of the Camp Fire Girls. Shea's original family home was in the Plum Creek Valley area, now beneath Chatfield Reservoir. *Courtesy Marlene Shea Thomas collection*

Louviers Cubs (Circa 1940). Chicago publisher William D. Boyce, lost in a London fog in 1909, was led to safety by a Scout doing a "good turn." Impressed, Boyce contacted Robert Baden-Powell, British founder, and then went back home to incorporate the Boy Scouts of America by 1910. By 1930, the BSA was helping younger

boys through Cub Scouting. Pictured here in the front row are Cubs Mike Shea, Raymond Kidder, and Ron Kidder, and in the back row, are Rod Richardson, Skip Hughes, Gus Lowell (Boy Scout), Danny Jones, and Bobby McCarthy. *Courtesy Marlene Shea Thomas private collection.*

A Community of Faith Forms (1927). In 1907, Rev. W. H. Schuruman, the Sunday School commissioner/missionary for the Presbyterian Board of Publication and Sabbath School Work, visited the Louviers tent camp. On Sunday, February 24, he returned to start a Sunday School, with Mrs. M. Armstrong as  superintendent. The Sabbath School met in a tent. If a minister was present, worship followed. In 1909, the Armstrongs moved away, and the Sabbath School ceased. In 1910, Rev. Schuruman, the Jack Family, and others started it up again. A room in the newly-erected school was set aside for church and social meetings. *Courtesy Mary Lee Rainey Johnston private collection.*

Church Life (Circa 1940). Louviers Community Presbyterian Church organized in 1927, with a building committee of Plant Superintendent E.R. Wright, O.S. DeLancy, George Park, and A. H. Orrison. Du Pont donated materials, and the people constructed the church, the only non-Du Pont structure in the town. Later, a steeple bell rang every Sunday. The sanctuary seated 65, and the basement held a kitchen and classrooms. Mary Lee Rainey, shown with her Sunday School, remembers gathering for a short time of song and worship. Those with birthdays dropped a penny for each year into the "birthday box," with each penny ringing a bell. *Courtesy Mary Lee Rainey Johnston private collection.*

Sunday Best (Circa 1940). Jackie and Skip Hughes, dressed for Easter Sunday, pose for a photograph in the triangle park of the "flats," the only park in Louviers. Children loved playing there. Marlene Shea Thomas remembers talking Wayne, Dick, or Denny Oblander, Skip Hughes, Butch Gelroth or her brother Mike Shea, into lifting her up into the "willow tree." Within minutes, she would want down, and she was too scared to jump. She'd yell for help, and one of the boys would lift her down. Du Pont held their annual company picnic in the park. *Courtesy of Marlene Shea Thomas private collection.*

The Willow Tree (Circa 1940). Vic, Elinor, Mike, Kathy, and little Marlene Shea pose near the willow tree. The "flat rats" played cowboys and Indians or "hide and seek" beneath its six-foot wide branches. "It was easy to climb because it had a knothole for your foot," said Marlene Thomas. "Then you would grab a branch and pull yourself up where there were two or three perfect places to sit and dream." Sometimes the children just talked or fantasized about going to New York. The county cut down the 75-year-old tree in 2003. A new young willow grows in the park for future tree-climbers to enjoy. *Courtesy Marlene Shea Thomas private collection.*

New Bikes! (October 1937). For their birthdays, Mary Lee and Sterling Rainey received matching Roadmaster bicycles. Their parents bought one, and the Cunningham grandparents, Aunt Ruth, Uncle Paul, Aunt Anna, and Uncle Clif bought the other one. The children were happy to finally own bicycles! Louviers was the kind of place where children could play safely and ask for a drink of water or Band-aid at any house. The village children were never allowed on the plant property, a rule devised for their safety. *Courtesy Mary Lee Rainey Johnston private collection.*

The School Playground (Circa 1935). A first school was rumored to be held early on in the "flats" area, but little information survives. Louviers District #36 was founded in June 1913, according to records in the State Archives, with the E.I. Du Pont de Nemours Company building the school for employees' children. One room held grades one through four, and one held grades five through eight. A third room was for activities, such as music or gym. All-school events were at the village clubhouse. After 1960-61, the school was demolished, with students moving to Plum Creek or Sedalia schools. *Courtesy Mary Lee Rainey Johnston private collection.*

**8th Grade Class--
Mary Lee and Five
Boys** (Circa 1940).
Mary Lee Rainey
Johnston went
through all eight
grades with the
same five boys,
shown here (L to
R): Billy Livingood,
Bill Arment,
George Livingood,
Albert Gelroth, and
James Hare. The
district-wide
graduation

ceremony for all 8th grade students was held in the Douglas County High School
auditorium in Castle Rock. Mary Lee won the Douglas County spelling contest held at
Douglas County High School when she was 13 years old, going on to the state
competition. *Courtesy Mary Lee Rainey Johnston private collection.*

**Douglas County
High School--
Graduationl** (May
1944). In 1897, high
school for area
students was in
Castle Rock. The
Cantril Building in
Castle Rock housed
a grade school and
high school. Most
Louviers high
school students
traveled daily to
Castle Rock or
boarded there; a
few went up to
Littleton High
School. The first
separate high school, built in 1907, burned in 1909 and was rebuilt out of rhyolite in 1910.
The stone high school was used until 1961, when the present DCHS was built on land
donated by the Scott family. *Courtesy Mary Lee Rainey Johnston private collection.*

Sunday Pastimes (Circa 1940). Earl and Nellie Cunningham relax outdoors on a sunny Sunday afternoon. Earl was foreman of the nitroglycerin division at Du Pont. The couple spent much time with their daughter and her family who lived next door. The local newspaper noted, "Mr. and Mrs. Earl Cunningham, Mr. and Mrs. Sterling Rainey and little daughter, motored to Colorado Springs." The little white dog in the photograph belonged to a boarder. He liked to chew Mary Lee Rainey's dolls and doll clothes, causing her much grief. *Courtesy Mary Lee Rainey Johnston private collection.*

Go, Du Pont! (Circa 1930). The plant team went to the Colorado State Softball Tournament one year, staying in the Vail Hotel in Pueblo. The hotel delivered pitchers of ice to rooms due to the heat. In this photo, Sterling Rainey is team manager. Lyman Bader, seated in front, was batboy. Clif Cunningham is in a vest and tie. Others in the photo

include: Paul Cunningham, Bunt Livingood, Del Colvin, Dud Clark and Charles Rennison. *Courtesy Mary Lee Rainey Johnston private collection.*

The Livingood Sweethearts (Circa 1942). Grandma and "Grandpa Bill" Livingood served fried chicken at a family picnic, which was a send-off for Hooney (George), Billy, and Burton, who were set to join the military service at Fort Logan. George had spots on his lungs, so he was turned down. Later on, the government exempted Du Pont workers from being drafted. From left

to right, Bill Livingood and Betty McCamlet Livingood, Floyd "Bunt" Livingood and Mildred Nichols Livingood; Lorretta Livingood Peterson and Pete Peterson, George Livingood and wife Beryl Hammond Livingood, and Frances Rudolph Livingood (now Harrison) and husband Burton Rudolph. *Courtesy Beryl Hammond Livingood private collection.*

Facing War-Time (1942). Billy Livingood, Burton Rudolph, and Hooney (George) Livingood pose for a photograph at the family picnic held before they left to join the service. During World War II, no planes were allowed to fly over the Du Pont operations at Louviers. Men on horseback patrolled the outer edge of the plant property. Also, even though Du Pont made explosives for mining and not for war, in the evenings, blackouts were required. Mrs. Elinor Shea remembers hearing the sound of the horse's hooves as a guard rode through town to make sure that all the shades were pulled down and the lights were off. *Courtesy Beryl Hammond Livingood private collection.*

A Family Town (Circa 1940). Louviers was a wonderful place to live, with Du Pont paying a good salary and providing housing and medical care. This young couple is George Livingood, fifth child of Bill and Pearl, and his wife Ida Beryl Hammond Livingood, originally from Larkspur. They pose here with baby Cheryl Lynn. Dana Earline came later in 1948. Their cousin's Ford is in the background. The parents and the daughters and their spouses all graduated from Douglas County High School, as did most of the other Livingood descendants. *Courtesy Beryl Hammond Livingood private collection.*

The Milk Man's Here! (Circa 1948). The Du Pont "company town" was self-contained, but the milk truck illustrates outside contact. Here, the Meadow Gold Milk truck driver delivers milk to Louviers' families on Coyote Row. The U.S. Patent Office granted the trademark name "Meadow Gold" to

the Continental Creamery Company of Topeka, Kansas in 1901. Continental and Beatrice Creamery merged in 1905. Later the name moved to out west, under Arden's Meadow Gold Dairy, and then Borden operations bought out Beatrice. In 1997, Southern Food Groups, Texas, bought Meadow Gold Dairies. *Courtesy of Douglas County History Research Center, Douglas County Libraries.*

The "Company Town" of Louviers at Mid-Century (Circa 1948). This aerial photograph shows mid-20th Century Louviers still thriving under the care of Du Pont. The population stood at around 350 people. Despite several tragic explosions over the years, Du Pont was known for its overall safety record. Du Pont operated the plant well into the 1980s. Another company leased it for approximately two years, and Du Pont took back the property, never to reopen it after 1986. In the early 1960s, Du Pont sold the company houses to residents and deeded town streets to the county. The fire hydrants and red fire boxes run by Du Pont were replaced in 1962 by the first fire truck. Three floods of the Plum Creek, in 1954, 1965, and 1973, destroyed town bridges and stranded residents for days. In 1999, the entire village was placed on the National Register of Historic Places thanks to the efforts of the Louviers Historical Foundation. In 2002, Du Pont donated 855 acres along Plum Creek to Douglas County for open space. Charles Jordan of The Conservation Fund lauded Du Pont for ensuring the "preservation of a cultural and natural oasis...our outdoor heritage." *X-12167Courtesy Denver Public Library, Western History Collection.*

Chapter Eight

Parker

The Twenty-Mile Landmark

by
Kathleen McCoy and Elizabeth Wallace

A Sketch of the Gold Region (Circa 1858-61). The actual date of this Gold Rush map is unknown, but it is believed to have been drawn between 1858-61. Although not to scale, the points of interest such as Denver City, Jimmy's Spring, Bent's Fort and the Cherokee Trail are clearly defined. Later, towns would spring up and become popular with travelers. One such town was Parker, where travelers could rest at the Twenty Mile House. Here they could replenish supplies, get repairs to their wagons and shoe livestock. Many families such as Parker, Tallman, Pouppirt, O'Brien, Newlin and the Clarke family played important roles in the development of Parker. Note the reference to Bent's Fort on the southeast edge of the map. The fort was strategically placed to maximize trading with various tribes of Native Americans. Brothers William and Charles Bent and a companion, Ceran St. Vrain, built the adobe fort in approximately 1830 and began trading with the Native Americans, notably the Cheyenne. William Bent eventually married a woman from the Cheyenne Tribe and, when she later passed away, he married her sister. William continued to manage the fort until it was abandoned in 1849. *I-19 Courtesy Colorado College Special Collections. (EW)*

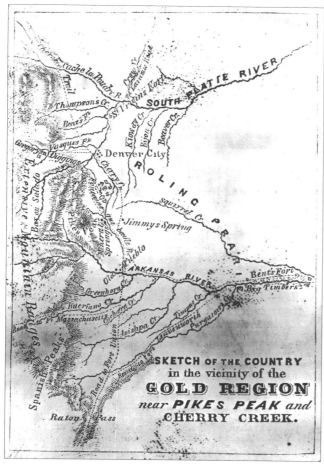

SKETCH OF THE COUNTRY in the vicinity of the GOLD REGION near PIKES PEAK and CHERRY CREEK.

A New Life Together (1897). In February 1897, William and Annie O'Brien were married in Leavenworth County, Kansas. Their first daughter, Modeste, was born while the couple lived in Kansas. William and Annie moved to Colorado hoping the curative air of the Rockies would improve William's health. Emma, their second child, was born while the couple lived at First Creek (east of Denver) where they were staying with Annie's brother, Emile Pouppirt. They moved to the Allison Ranch in Parker in 1900. The Allison Ranch had two two-story houses, which, in 1893, opened, as a resort catering to health seekers mainly those suffering from tuberculosis and other respiratory diseases. Annie and William managed the houses, where Annie cooked and William farmed. Their first son, Charles, was born there in 1901. They purchased 360 acres east of the Allison Ranch, where William built a three-bedroom farmhouse. They gave up the management of the Allison Ranch. Their second son William Leslie (Les) was born in their farmhouse in 1903, followed by a daughter, Lorraine, in 1913. William began supporting his growing family as a carpenter, while farming his own land. *Courtesy Jean Martin. (EW)*

Moving On (Circa 1930). In 1919 William and Annie O'Brien sold their farm to Mr. X.J. Bauldauf and purchased the home of Dr. Walter Heath seen in this photograph. In this large house, Annie took in boarders to supplement the family's income. William continued practicing his trade of carpentry. He was well known in the Parker area as a quality builder. Jean Martin said, "…many of the houses and businesses in Parker reflect the workmanlike construction that was his trademark." The O'Brien's younger children attended the new Parker Consolidated School, where, for a time, William served on the school board. *Courtesy Jean Martin. (EW)*

Later in Life (Circa 1930). The O'Briens pose for this photograph much later in their lives. Note the formal manner in which Mr. O'Brien is standing. His granddaughter, Jean Martin remembers that her grandfather loved having his photograph taken and would always "…stand up straight and look directly at the camera…he was a studious man…" During their marriage, William and Annie had five children one of whom William Leslie (Les), decided to purchase the farm his father had sold to Mr. Bauldauf in 1919. After buying the ranch, Les and his wife Eunice improved it, adding a new barn and a chicken house. *Courtesy Jean Martin. (EW)*

Twenty-Mile House (Circa 1890). The town of Parker was originally known as Pine Grove. The history of the Twenty Mile House began with a small one-room building that was owned by Alfred Butters. He traded the property to Mr. Goldsmith, who then sold it to Mr. Long. In 1865, George Long had the home moved from its original location in Pine Grove about one mile north. He added 10 rooms to the property and also an upper floor making the Twenty-Mile House an important stop for travelers on the Cherokee Trail. *92011 Courtesy Douglas County History Research Center, Douglas County Libraries. (EW)*

An Ensemble (Date unknown). The Parker Band was featured in the "Weekly Mascot" paper as early as 1899 for Denver's music week. They played for an enthusiastic audience in front of the Knight Campbell Music Company and the May company. Next, they performed at the Fitzsimmons Hospital for disabled patients, followed by a radio program on the Fitzsimmons station KFUP. A.G. Russell of Denver photographed the Parker band musicians playing a cello, horn, guitar and violins. *666.05 Courtesy Douglas Country History Research Center, Douglas County Libraries. (KM)*

The Smithy (Circa 1900). As with many pioneering towns, businesses sprang up to meet the needs of the homesteaders. A general store, post office and a blacksmith shop often appeared as the first establishments in a town. Edith Parker Low, daughter of James and Mattie Parker, remembers many interesting incidents from her childhood. "My father operated a blacksmith shop in connection with the hotel, and these oxen had to be shod, as well as horses. The process was different however, as the oxen had to be suspended in the air by means of a wide belt which swung from a four-posted scaffolding and was operated by a pulley. Mexicans drove these teams, as a rule, and they usually had a goat or two riding on top of the load in order to have milk..." Edith recalls a time when her family had a strange guest to dinner one night. "...on one occasion [there] was a man who kept a small black silk cap on his head. We were told that he had been scalped in an Indian raid, escaping with his life—something quite unusual." *666.01Courtesy Douglas County History Research Center, Douglas County Libraries. (EW)*

Riding the Ranch (Circa 1930). Ed Pouppirt bought thousands of acres in the Parker area and raised cattle and horses. Lorraine M. O'Brien recalls that a windmill provided water for the house and for the horse and dairy cattle – water could be pumped directly into the stock tanks or into a storage tank that was set 10 or 14 feet above ground. It is believed that Ed maintained a herd that varied in size from 400 to 800 head, although, for one reason or another, many ranchers never revealed the actual size of their herds. *Courtesy Jean Martin. (EW)*

Happy Days (Circa 1920-3). Mrs. Jean Martin, daughter of Modeste, who was the first child of Annie and William O'Brien, believes Lorraine O'Brien, youngest of the O'Brien children probably took the above photograph, since she is not in the picture and this photo came from

her personal album. The family is gathered in front of Ed and Lena Pouppirt's house. Back L to R): Lena (Kern) Pouppirt, Ed Pouppirt, Emma (Pouppirt) Sargent, Annie (Pouppirt) O'Brien, Shirley (Fletcher) Pouppirt, holding son Fletcher Pouppirt, Modeste Pouppirt. Front (L to R): Unidentified, unidentified, Modeste Pouppirt, Jr. Wayne Pouppirt, (sons of Modeste and Shirley). *Courtesy Jean Martin. (EW)*

An Excellent Horsewoman (1904). Ed and Lena Pouppirt pose for the camera on their wedding day. After their marriage, they lived in Denver while Ed's brother-in-law, William O'Brien, built their new home in Parker. The Pouppirts were one of the first in the area to light their home with acetylene gas. During their lifetime, the Pouppirt's acquired more than 7,000 acres of farm and rangeland in Douglas and Arapahoe Counties, including the property on which the old Twenty Mile House was located. When Lena was a young girl, her parents, Max and Anna Margaret Kern, sent her to Germany to complete her schooling, including music. She was also a competent horsewoman who rode a willful mare called Lady. Lena loved to cook and so gathered wild fruit including plums, chokecherries and currants, all of which she used to make jellies and jams. Ed and Lena never had children of their own, but Mrs. Martin recalls their house was a fun place to visit and "…was always full of nieces and nephews." *Courtesy Jean Martin. (EW)*

From Horse and Buggy to Automobile (Circa 1938). Ed and Lena Pouppirt stand next to their Model A Ford, having made the change from horse and buggy to automobile. Edward was born in Leavenworth, Kansas, in 1870, of French parents, and moved to Douglas County in 1901. Lena was born in 1876. Her parents, Max and Anna Margaret Kern, were ranchers in Arapahoe County, Colorado. According to one of their nieces, Lorraine M. O'Brien, Ed and Lena often had their "...nieces and nephews who might come to visit for a weekend, or for the summer or winter." The couple had a state-of-the-art home including a "dumb waiter" where Lena could choose from her supplies in the cellar, place them on a tray, and use a pulley system to bring them up to the pantry. Their home was also one of the first in the area to be lit by acetylene gas. Ed and Lena were active members of Cherry Creek Grange as well as other community activities. Ed died in 1942 and Lena passed away in 1960. *Courtesy Jean Martin. (EW)*

© Colorado Historical Society

First Pine Grove--Then Parker *(Between 1868-1887).* In 1868, James Parker married Mattie Haynes Wallace, a young widow with two young daughters and settled in Pine Grove (later renamed Parker). In 1870, James purchased the Twenty-Mile House, an important resting place for travelers. Mattie and James had a daughter, Edith, who is believed to have been the favorite child of James. Evidence of his favoritism toward his youngest daughter was shown when he suggested the name of Pine Grove should be changed to Edithville. In 1881 there were two towns in Colorado called Pine Grove and since this caused some confusion with the Post Office, the name needed to be changed. However, the Post Office refused the name of Edithville and decided to use the name of Parker instead. In 1887, Mattie died and James married the local schoolteacher, Eva. Evidently poor Eva did not make the grade as far as the girls were concerned, because they nicknamed her "Mugger." When the three girls grew to womanhood, they married young men from the Parker area. In 1910, James Parker sold his property to Charles P. Mety and moved to Denver, where he died in December of that year. *10025192 Courtesy Colorado Historical Society, Western History Collection. (EW)*

Coyote Chorus (1925). Elizabeth and John Tallman, early residents of Parker, pose for the camera. Elizabeth remembers her first visit to the Twenty-Mile House. "My sister and I stayed all night at the first house built in Parker, then (known as) the Twenty-Mile House, built by a man named Long…We were the first travelers to stop there, and Mr. and Mrs. Long had to sleep out-of-doors as we had their bed…the coyote chorus kept the dog barking so that we could not sleep, but after a time, he quieted down. The next morning I asked Mrs. Long about the dog. She said 'I got up and hung the little devil…'" *CHS10031672 Courtesy Colorado Historical Society, Western History Collection. (EW)*

Curious About the Settlers (Date Unknown). There are many stories of Native Americans being curious of the white settlers' habits and customs. The Native Americans would often arrive when the lady of the house was cooking biscuits, which they seemed to favor. Mrs. Young, a homesteader, recalls a band begging for food one day. Since she was just about to discard a batch of

biscuits in which she had used too much soda, she decided to offer those to them instead. They thought the biscuits were delicious and continued on their way. *B-13 Courtesy Colorado College Special Collections. (EW)*

SCENERY.

Bartering (Circa 1870). Chief Washington, seen in this photograph with his wife, was known to visit Parker at least once a year. Elizabeth Tallman recalls an incident with Ute Chief Washington when he came to town "…at one time old Washington and his band were in camp near when there came a heavy snowstorm. My brother was looking for cattle and found an old squaw all alone some distance from camp, nearly frozen. She was Washington's mother. My brother took her to camp and demanded why Washington did not care for her. His reply was, 'Too old; no work. Heap no bueno.' What finally became of her we never knew." Elizabeth remembers another incident when Chief Washington wanted to trade some ponies for Elizabeth's then two-year-old son. "Washington pointed to the little fellow and said 'Swap ponies?' and held up two fingers. I said 'no swap'. Then he held up three fingers and I shook my head. He kept on adding a pony at a time until he had offered twenty ponies. He was very much disgusted when I would not accept such a good trade." *X-30645 Courtesy Colorado Historical Society, Western History Collection. (EW)*

Play Ball (Circa 1910-1920). Left to right Rear: Billy Ellis, Richard Hawkey, Ernest (Bud) Jewell, C. Montgomery, A Herzog, Otis Tillery. Front left to right: Sweet, Childs, Dack Baldauf; Edgar Montgomery. It is generally believed the game of baseball was derived from an English game called Rounders.

However, in 1845 an enterprising man called Cartwright devised an American version. He modified the rules to include nine players, instigated the "three outs rule", changed the distance between bases to 90 feet, and arranged the bases in a diamond formation. *66604 Courtesy Douglas County History Research Center, Douglas County Libraries. (EW)*

Poetry for Cows (Circa 1926-28). Brothers, Harry and Charles Clarke kept cattle in Cripple Creek. For spending money, they would sell hay and one winter there was not enough hay for the cattle. As a result, the Clarkes bought a good hay-producing ranch where Stroh Ranch development now stands. Pictured is

another brother, Roy; he ranched and worked on the Colorado & Southern Railroad for $2.50 a day. He also worked in the family lumber and hardware store, which was originally owned by John Oswald, then bought by the Clarke family in 1916. Roy was fondly remembered for reciting poetry while milking cows. *Courtesy Gertrude Clarke Kordziel. (KM)*

Ranch Hand Unknown (Circa 1928-29). Horses were the most utilized animals on a homestead. They were a source of power for working the farm and acted as transportation to school, church or the local saloon. Horses also herded cattle and even moved houses by  hauling the buildings over poles as it was rolled along. In the United States, the horse population peaked in the early 1900s. The back of this photo does not identify the ranch hand, but these valued horses' names were recorded as the following (L to R): Jim, Diamond, Lady and Shorty. *Courtesy Gertrude Clarke Kordziel. (KM)*

Searching for Gold (Circa 1930-33). Parker had its own gold rush days and the Clarke family collected enough to pay the bills for the farm, during 1929-1933. They would collect gold on the west side of Cherry Creek, but sometimes gold was discovered in the craw of a butchered chicken. Roy Clarke remarked when housing was being developed in Parker with this, "They are sitting on a gold mine and don't even know it." Pictured front row (L to R): Wilma and Ruth, middle row (L to R): Mary Clarke holding Charlotte, back row (L to R): Charles Roley, Roy Clarke and Garnett Roley. *Courtesy Gertrude Clarke Kordziel. (KM)*

A Favorite Pastime (Circa 1930-33). The "carpet" method was used by the Clarkes when collecting gold. The collection was deposited on an old carpet, and when it was tilted the heavy gold would settle into the fibers. Next a sluice-box, a sloping trough, was used to further separate the elements, as water rushed over them. The Clarkes dug into the bank of Cherry Creek and piped creek or spring water for the separation process. Pictured (L to R): Roy Clarke, Garnett Roley, Mary Clarke, holding Charlotte with Wilma on left and Ruth on right in front, then Charles Roley. *Courtesy Gertrude Clarke Kordziel. (KM)*

A Riderless Horse (Circa 1900). The feed and livery store is pictured center in downtown Parker. These establishments were crucial to railroad travelers, who would hire a horse and buggy once they arrived. Horses could be boarded, but when Roy Clarke worked for the Colorado & Southern, he would

ride his horse the three miles to the rail, and then send his riderless horse home. Seven-year-old daughter, Ruth, would then ride it back to meet him after work. Also, downtown was the family's lumber and hardware company, located on the north side of Main Street, east of the Twenty-Mile House Monument. *Courtesy Gertrude Clarke Kordziel. (KM)*

A Bee Keeper (Circa 1954). Mary A. Deal Clarke came from Bird City, Kansas. After losing their homestead, Mary's father abandoned her mother; consequently, Mary and her three siblings were placed in an orphanage for six years. Mary liked to cook, sew and keep bees. When the family moved to the Twin Houses, they farmed the black bottom land that was good soil for corn. After Mary married Roy, they started their own herd of cattle with four cows and used the Bell Cross brand from her family, registered since 1918. Today's Bell Cross Ranch has a road in her name, Mary Clarke Circle. *Courtesy Gertrude Clarke Kordziel. (KM)*

Medal Winner (1978). LeRoy G. Clarke was born in Seneca, Illinois September 19, 1903. He later lived in California and demonstrated his athletic ability by winning the California Decathlon Medal in 1920. He came to Parker in 1925 and ranched the Stroh area. The entrance to Bell Cross Ranch is named after him. He also raised beef cattle on a ranch where Parker Pine Lane Elementary and Homestead Hills is located. He met his wife Mary, who lived in one of the Twin Houses, out in the field by fixing the broken rein on her horse's bridle. *Courtesy Gertrude Clarke Kordziel. (KM)*

133

Community Spirit (1950). The Parker Community Center was completed in 1951. It was run by volunteers and used for dances, serving hot lunches and community meetings, but mostly it was used for basketball. Parker had become known for its dedication to the  sport and after its completion, Parker High School began using it for their practices and games. In the 1940s, the students played in a railroad shed. Gertrude Clarke Kordziel said the athletes used to complain of the splinters they had to remove after playing ball in that shed. *Courtesy Gertrude Clarke Kordziel. (KM)*

Twin Houses (1928). In the background of this photo are the "Twin Houses," built by F.H. Allison in 1885. Later known as Ponce de Leon Chalybeate Springs sanitarium, its mineral springs attracted tuberculosis patients from the east coast. One building was moved four miles north of Parker and turned into a boutique shop. The other remains on its original site at the southeast corner of Parker and Stroh Roads and is used as a barn. Pictured in the foreground (L to R): Charles Roley, unknown, Pete Sanchez, Isom Roley and Roy Clarke on the tractor. *Courtesy Gertrude Clarke Kordziel. (KM)*

Chapter Nine

Roxborough Park

A Great Place to Drive Dull Cares Away

by
Susan Trumble

Roxborough--Home and Hunting Ground Throughout Time (Circa 1910). The beautiful red sandstone spires of Roxborough have attracted people for thousands of years. The rock formations provided a place of shelter. High points served as lookouts for hunting game animals. Fresh water springs offered water and encouraged a variety of plant foods. Archaeological evidence of the earliest people dates back over 5000 years. The Arapahoe and Cheyenne made this area home until they were relocated onto reservations in 1872. The Ute people roamed the area until the early 1880s. *Courtesy Roxborough State Park.*

A Place Picturesque (Circa 1910). "The woodless plain is terminated by a range of naked and almost perpendicular rocks, visible at a distance of several miles and resembling a vast wall parallel to the base of the mountain with

interesting views of singular color and formation, the whole scenery truly picturesque and romantic." Dr. Edwin James, a scientist with the Stephen Long Expedition of 1820 recorded these thoughts of Roxborough, as the mission neared the mouth of the South Platte River near present day Waterton. *Courtesy Roxborough State Park.*

Cattle and Cultivation--A Way of Life (Circa 1910). Farming and cattle ranching became economic mainstays to early settlers in Roxborough. Denis S. Cooper received one of the first land patents in July 1871 for 160 acres. He reported constructing a log home 14 feet by 14 feet with one window and one door. The documents record that he had five acres under cultivation and built more that 20 rods of pole and post fence. Most of the homestead claims at Roxborough date back to the period between 1870 and 1890. *Courtesy Roxborough State Park.*

Henry Persse--an Enthusiastic Proponent (Circa 1910). Henry Stratford Persse came from an Irish family who believed in the American dream. His grandfather, a member of the respected Persse family of County Galway, sent Henry's father and two uncles to America to find their fortune. They became successful farmers and merchants in New York and endowed Henry with a love of America and a "can-do" attitude. Henry Persse was a wool grower, brewer and merchant in New York before Colorado captured his attention. Mr. Persse traveled across the plains from his home in New York to Colorado over 26 times, between 1880 and 1890. He wrote articles for the New York newspapers recounting the beauty and opportunity to be found in Colorado. By 1890 Mr. Persse moved permanently to Denver, bringing with him his wife Ruby, and adult children, John, Horace, Amelia and Mary Anna. In Colorado, Mr. Persse was involved in a variety of mining and real estate ventures. *Courtesy Roxborough State Park.*

Roxborough--the "City" of Rocks (Circa 1910). The name "Roxborough" was given to this land by Henry Stratford Persse about 1900. The Persse ancestral estate in County Galway, Ireland bore this name and Henry found it fitting for this place of amazing rock formations. Mr. Persse became part owner of land at Roxborough when Edward Griffith defaulted on a loan reportedly stating "that a bunch of rocks in Colorado were not worth paying the taxes on." Persse later bought out Griffith's partners. *Courtesy Roxborough State Park.*

ROXBOROUGH PARK, COLO.

Persse "Country Home" (Circa 1910). Henry Persse built a "country home" at Roxborough of locally quarried native Lyons sandstone. He used the home as headquarters to entertain prominent guests from Denver. Some of the old homestead structures built 30 years before by Denis Cooper became outbuildings for the Persse Place. One of the outbuildings contains Henry S. Persse's name, the date of 1903 and a variety of interesting philosophical inscriptions.

> *A new broom sweeps clean--an old one has a sweeping tale to unfold.*

> *God blesses the man who helps himself and d---- the man who helps himself here.*

> *It is not what a man does that is important but how he comes out of it.*

Henry's son John, a retired Denver police officer, lived on the property full time from 1907 until his death in 1937. He raised crops, chickens and cattle. Children growing up in the area remember John Persse as a congenial neighbor who would give them candy when they came to visit. Today, the Persse Place can be visited on the Fountain Valley Trail at Roxborough State Park. The stone house was restored in 1996 and two of the log outbuildings are currently under restoration with assistance from the Colorado Historical Fund. *Courtesy Roxborough State Park.*

Early Industry (Circa 1910). Henry Persse owned the mineral rights to clay and silica found in the Dakota Hogback at Roxborough. These raw materials were mined for the manufacture of building bricks. The Silicated Brick Company operated from 1904 until 1912. It went into bankruptcy and was reformed as the Silica Brick and Clay Company, which continued to manufacture bricks until 1916. According to Robert Woodhouse, in the book *Douglas County, A Historical Journey,* "these bricks were made from a mixture of ground lime rock and silica sand. As they were made they were placed on small cars and pushed into a long steel boiler. At night the boiler was shut up tightly and steam turned on. These bricks were not baked but steamed with high pressure steam." The bricks produced by the Silica Brick and Clay Company were white with a large "S" imprinted on them. The bricks were shipped into Denver by a branch line of the Colorado and Southern Railroad known as the "Silica Branch" and used in building construction throughout the region. *Courtesy Roxborough State Park.*

Mining for Clay and Silica (Circa 1910). Providing the raw materials and manufacturing the bricks required a significant work force. Twenty-seven men were listed as employed by the Silicated Brick Company in the United States Census of 1910. The miners were a diverse group of men ranging in age

from 19 to 69. Although many came from mid-western states there were also men from New York, Florida and Texas. These laborers were American born, unlike the Silica Company's Board of Directors, who were English transplants to this country. *Courtesy Roxborough State Park.*

Silica--Now Silent (Circa 1910). The town of Silica grew up around the brick plant. Most of the homes of the married miners' families were simple clapboard construction. The single men working as laborers lived at a boarding house run by Elizabeth Sobey Lewis. She cooked for as many as 45 people at a rate of $5 per week. Silica became a ghost town after the closing of the Silica Brick and Clay Company in 1916. The company's assets were sold at a sheriff's auction in 1917 and the land was later acquired by the Helmer family. All that remains today is the kiln used for steaming the bricks. *Courtesy, Roxborough State Park.*

School Days (Circa 1910). The Douglas County District Nineteen School operated from sometime before 1898 until 1948. Twenty-four children from the local Roxborough mining and ranching families were enrolled in 1910. Names found in the school register include Allen, Campbell, Childers, Frauenhoff, Helmer, Waterhouse and Woodard. As was the case with many small country schools at the time, the one-room school included grades one through eight. The School Board was comprised of local residents who hired the teacher and oversaw the school's operation. The 1910 school census for District Nineteen was certified by Horace Persse and Homer Childers. The average tenure of teachers was relatively short. The teachers often lived with local families. Among those who taught at Roxborough were Bell Hooton, Ollie Woodard, Theda Cooper, Anna Freeland and Mrs. George (Hazel) Helmer. After the school closed, the building was moved to George Helmer's ranch headquarters. The foundation of the school is still visible east of the intersection of Rampart and Waterton Roads. *Courtesy Roxborough State Park.*

A Great Place to Drive Dull Cares Away (Circa 1910). Henry Persse invited many of Denver's elite to visit his country home amid the red rocks. Governor James B. Grant gave Mr. Persse a guest book on the occasion of his 70th birthday in 1907. The book records the sentiments of Henry's guests.

A great place to drive dull cares away

James B. Grant 1907

A grand place to study the Wonders of Nature

Charles A. Kendrick 1908

Not "Garden of the Gods" but grander "God's Garden"

Frank Wickersham 1909

A golden link in memory's chain

Mrs. John F. Campion 1905

Should be owned by the City of Denver for the free use of the people

Mayor Robert Spear 1910

Courtesy Roxborough State Park.

Poetry and Post Cards (Circa 1910). In addition to the guest book, Mr. Persse made a series of post cards from which many of these photographs originate. This poem to "Persse's Sandstone Dells" was found on the back of one of the postcards.

Post Card.

THIS SIDE FOR ADDRESS ONLY.

PLACE
ONE CENT STAMP
HERE

Roxborough Park.

There's a place between the foot hills
  And the level, sea-like plain,
Where the peaks loom high behind you
  And in front waves golden grain;
'Taint quite high enough for many,
  Nor quite low enough for some;
But it's here I've built my cabin,
  Far from strife-filled cities hum.

Here the range, behind is golden
  With the glowing light of day;
And the prairie's like a painting,
  Where the last warm sunbeams lay;
And along the dimpled stretches--
  Humble hints of grander heights--
Falls a magic veil of purple
  From those fading, dying lights.

Seem's if some folks can't be suited
  'Cept upon the highest peak;
And still others, on the lowlands,
  Must their fame and fortune seek;
But right here's the happy medium
  And it's here contentment dwells,
When the afternoon is dying
  'Mongst the Persse's sandstone dells.

Courtesy Roxborough State Park

144

Resort Dreams (Circa 1910). Mr. Persse invited members of Denver's elite to visit his home amid the rocks. Roxborough's popularity grew as a favorite "outing place." An article in the Denver Republican of January 21, 1907 predicted...

> *By August of this year, electric cars will be running from Denver to an all-year-round resort south of the city that promises to rival in attractiveness anything else the state can boast. A first-class hotel, golf links, a club house, a well stocked lake, charming driveways, and comfortable cottages all placed in surroundings said to be the most beautiful, these will form the attractions of Roxborough park, natural beauty spot located in the hills near Plum Creek.*

> *It will be a first class resort in every respect...The hotel will be of white silica brick with 20 foot porches, a large ballroom, billiard rooms and all the other appurtenances of a resort hotel.*

Courtesy Roxborough State Park.

From Resort to Ranch (Circa 1910). The beauty of Roxborough continued to inspire Mr. Persse's guests for years to come. Henry Persse's guest book records visits through 1917 from members of Denver's elite including such notables as Mayor Speer, the Phipps, Grant and Crawford Hill families. Henry died in a streetcar accident in 1918 and with him went his dreams for a first-class resort at Roxborough. The property was purchased by the Helmer family and returned to ranching operations. *Courtesy Roxborough State Park.*

Helmer Headquarters (Circa 1950). Frank Helmer and his son Anton homesteaded property in the Roxborough area in 1876. Over the next 90 years, the family bought out many of the local landowners including the Persses. As a result the Helmer's holdings grew to over 3,000 acres. Anton's sons, George and Toney supervised the mining and cattle operation. Even though the brick factory closed, the Helmer Brothers continued to mine clay and silica and shipped it into Denver for brick making. The Helmer Brothers were known throughout the country for their highly prized Hereford show cattle raised here.

The photo shows Toney Helmer's ranch headquarters as it looked in 1950. Several of the buildings had been part of the town of Silica. The barn at the upper right had been a general store during the brickyard days. It was later used for barn dances by the Helmers. The brickyard superintendent's home to the far right later became the Toney Helmer family residence. *Courtesy Roxborough State Park.*

147

From Ranch to Roxborough State Park (Circa 1910). In 1975, Colorado State Parks began to acquire land at Roxborough which would eventually be opened to the public as Roxborough State Park in 1987. The park has grown to over 3,300 acres and is recognized as a National Archaeological District, a National Natural Landmark and a Colorado Natural Area. The park now hosts over 100,000 visitors each year. Many of these current guests echo the sentiments recorded nearly 100 years ago by Governor Grant, a visit to Roxborough Park is a "great way to drive dull cares away." *Courtesy Roxborough State Park.*

Chapter Ten

Sedalia

Town at the Crossroads

by
Laura Adema

Sedalia Began as Round Corral (Circa 1890). The earliest settlers formed a town above the junction of East and West Plum Creek. John H. Craig and a few friends built a cattle pen there and called it "Corral" or "Round Corral." The corral was slightly southwest of present day Sedalia, alongside the First Territorial Road, carrying travelers between Denver and Colorado City. Early settlers of the area included John H. Craig and Jonathon House. In 1871, the Denver & Rio Grande Railroad finished its narrow gauge railroad tracks and built a depot called Plum Station. The name may have come from an abundance of plum trees located near the creek. The Town of Plum was platted in 1873 by the National Land and Improvement Company. Pictured above is an early view of Sedalia, showing a pile of railroad ties in the foreground and a wide dirt road behind. Two riders on horseback are racing down the street just below a sign that reads "Corral." The front porch on the left is the Weaver House, built in 1881. It was a hotel that supported the livery stable and corral.
Courtesy Louise Beeman Hier.

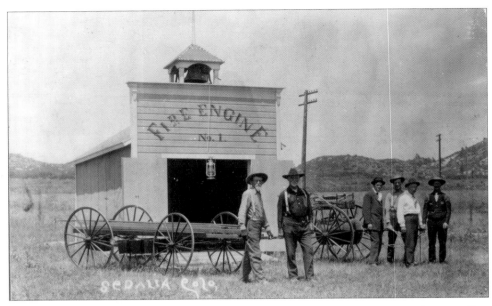

Manpower Pulls Early Fire Equipment (Circa 1907). The Sedalia Volunteer Fire Department was established in 1907. Pictured are volunteer fire fighters next to two pieces of hand drawn fire equipment. The apparatus at right is a chemical fire extinguisher. The tank held water mixed with baking soda. When acid was added to the tank, a chemical reaction occurred. The water, under pressure, could be used to put out a fire. This fire station was torn down when US Highway 85 was realigned and connected to state Highway 67. *687.016 Courtesy Douglas County History Research Center, Douglas County Libraries.*

Where there's Smoke (April 1924). The Beeman children pose in front of their Sedalia home. Florence, Louise and Jack are in front with Harriett and Annie in back. One morning their mother, Harriett Beeman, found smoke coming from under a bedroom door. A fire, started in a wood stove grew out of control. Harriett saved her children by handing them over the fence to a neighbor. When the fire department's chemical tank arrived, it was empty. The house burned to the ground. It is not surprising that Harriett became active in the volunteer fire department. *Courtesy Louise Beeman Hier.*

Let's go to Town (Circa 1915). The George Manhart Store, built in 1889, was a popular destination for ranchers in the Sedalia area. The first floor consisted of a post office and grocery store. George and Betty Manhart lived behind the store until their twelfth child was born. In the center is Mr. Merrell the station agent, holding the hand of his daughter Harriett. The man in the white shirt is Albert Manhart with his children Thomas Albert and Ashton. Burt Perry is on the far right end. *687.019 Courtesy Douglas County History Research Center, Douglas County Libraries.*

Demolished after Ninety-Eight Years (Circa 1915). The grocery business made George Manhart a rich man with trade generating $3,500 a month. His success was due to the quality of his service and the two railroads that ran through the town of Sedalia. The town folk gathered on the second floor of this building for various community activities including a Thanksgiving dinner and dance held in 1927. (Rocky Mountain News, December 4, 1987, pg. 40). The store was torn down in 1987 after the county condemned the building. *687.545 Courtesy Douglas County History Research Center, Douglas County Libraries.*

Julia Francis Paddison Curtis (Circa 1863). Born in Wales and married at age 22, Julia is pictured here eight years before coming to America in 1871. An industrious woman, Julia would soon find herself challenged by pioneer life in Colorado. Homesteading near Sedalia, they called their ranch "Oaklands." When they arrived the farmhouse on the property had only three rooms. Four rooms were added to accommodate the nine children that traveled with them to America. Julia churned butter, gathered eggs, chased coyotes and raised a large family without modern conveniences. She died in 1913 at the age of eighty-six. *Courtesy Denna Garcilaso Torres*

Henry Harper Curtis (Circa 1863). Born in Wales, September 5, 1830, Henry Harper Curtis was a successful jeweler. He moved to Australia in 1849 and made a small fortune either buying or finding gold. He returned to Wales and dreamed of America. It was not poverty but a spirit of adventure that led Henry to America. He traveled by ship to New York and by train to Colorado. The story of Henry and Julia's trip to America is preserved in the form of family letters dated 1871-72. Henry helped build St. Phillip in the Field Episcopal Church, south of Sedalia. *Courtesy Denna Garcilaso Torres*

Home on the Range (Circa 1890). Oaklands was established in 1871 on the east bank of West Plum Creek. The original 160 acres grew over the years to 560 acres to accommodate the increasing dairy herd. The farm produced wheat, oats and potatoes. Julia Curtis made 100 pounds of high quality butter per week and sold it for forty cents a pound. In 1971, the Curtis' 100-year family reunion was held on the ranch. Five hundred invited guests danced on Friday night and picnicked on Saturday. *Courtesy Denna Garcilaso Torres.*

Excerpt from Henry Harper Curtis' personal letters – On board the ship "Java" traveling to America
(1871).

My Dear Brother,

We have now been a week at sea and have traveled nearly two-thirds of the journey to America. The voyage so far, has been tolerably pleasant, but Tuesday and Wednesday were very rough indeed, the sea was washing over the bows every two or three minutes, and the greater part of the passengers unable to leave their berths. I was the only one of our family able to be about, and although I am a good sailor, the sight and sound of so many sick people nearly knocked me over, and I suffered a good deal from a headache but continued to keep about and assist those in distress. We have some very pleasant companions on board, in the salon nearly the whole of them Americans; we find them kind and communicative, with none of the obtrusive inquisitiveness generally attributed to Americans.... They all agree that Colorado is a fine state to go to, and we cannot fail to do well there.

Eight Children and Eight Grades (Circa 1936). Oaklands School was located one mile south of the Curtis ranch at the corner of Wolfensberger Road and Highway 105. The students were primarily from the Curtis family. Front row: (L to R) Donna, Gwen, Ron and Dave Curtis. Back row: Bob and Mildred Curtis, Irene Klug and Vera Griffith. Dave Curtis has fond memories of Edna Jean Manhart as his teacher, praised by all as an excellent instructor. In 1988 the school district moved the building to its present location next to South Elementary School in Castle Rock. *Courtesy David A. and Carol Curtis.*

Church With a Story (2004). Newton S. Grout was the main carpenter for this small community church built in 1872. He fashioned the church after a small church in Maine where he worshiped as a child. In 1888, John Harris was hired to add a vestibule on the east side and sacristy on the west side. Eastern red cedar was used to finish the interior of the building. With the help of other West Plum Creek settlers, the building was completed and consecrated on November 5, 1889, as St. Phillip in the Field Episcopal Church by Bishop Spaulding. The church is located five miles south of Sedalia on Perry Park Road. The Bear Canon Cemetery, surrounding the church, was also started by early settlers. *Derald Hoffman, photographer.*

An Apple a Day (Circa 1900). In 1896, William T. Lambert organized a family venture--an orchard, on his ranch west of Sedalia. He planted 28,000 trees, a combination of apple, cherry and plum. He also stocked 400,000 saplings in the nursery. The "Lambert Orchard Company" prospered for many years. The family designed the trademark and packaging. Products for sale were apple butter, cider and juice. Neighbors came to pick their own fruit. The orchard ultimately failed, but the ranching operation continued to prosper. *Courtesy Frances Lambert Prescott/Copy at the Sedalia Historic Fire House Museum L2.*

Back Breaking Work (Circa 1900). In 1894, William T. Lambert planted a large orchard. Providing water was the challenge. Lambert first dug a well 900 feet deep. He attached a windmill and built a reservoir on the hilltop above the orchard. A dam, built on Indian Creek, filled the reservoir with water. A series of pipes were laid to carry water from the reservoir and rubber hoses brought water to the trees. The Colorado weather and short growing season finally ruined the great venture. The company was dissolved around 1914. *Courtesy of Frances Lambert Prescott/copy at The Sedalia Historic Fire House Museum. L21.*

155

First Church in Sedalia (October 1921). The Sedalia Community Presbyterian Church was built at the junction of East and West Plum Creek, on land donated by Fred Crangle. In 1919, the forerunner to the church was called the Sedalia Sabbath School. The building was dedicated on October 23, 1921. This was the first official church to be completed in Sedalia. The new church quickly became the spiritual hub of the community. On January 22, 1922 Reverend A.G. Beecham became the permanent minister for the church. Sadly, the great flood of 1965 washed this building away. *Courtesy New Hope Presbyterian Church.*

I Do, Do You? (October 1922). One year after The Sedalia Community Presbyterian Church opened, a double wedding took place. The wedding featured Curtis brothers marrying Crangle sisters. The ceremony took place on Tuesday, October 10, 1922. Pictured above, shortly after the ceremony are (front) Charlie and Bess Curtis and (back) Ed and Beulah Curtis. The newlyweds are enjoying their new Mitchell six-cylinder convertible. Both couples moved into the Curtis homestead and lived together for the rest of their lives. Close family members say that they never seemed to fight. *Courtesy David A. and Carol Curtis.*

US Cavalry Camped Near Sedalia (Circa 1895). Fort Logan records show Sedalia was an overnight campsite for troops marching to target practice in Perry Park and Colorado Springs. The first group camped in Sedalia on July 9, 1895. Nine officers and 200 enlisted men traveled together. They marched 15 miles in one day to reach Sedalia and set up camp next to the water tank of the Denver & Rio Grande Railroad. The fields west of Sedalia were used by the troops for about three years. *687.001 Courtesy Douglas County History Research Center, Douglas County Libraries.*

Two Patriots (Circa 1918). Charles and Henry Curtis are dressed in their military uniforms near the end of World War I. They served together stateside, working as mechanics repairing seaplanes for about seven months. The first Marine Corp Air Division was established in 1912. They were disappointed not to serve on the front lines, but they may have underestimated their vital role in keeping the planes in the air. They returned home November 6, 1918. *Courtesy David A. and Carol Curtis.*

Do We Have To Go? (Circa 1912). The Sedalia school was part of the pioneer school district. Classes began in 1865. A wooden schoolhouse was built in 1878. The student population outgrew that school so a new one was built, adding a windmill, water tank and flagpole. An influx of families to the canyon created a need for a second addition to the school in 1912, doubling its size. The school appears in many Sedalia pictures which is helpful in "dating" pictures by looking at the size and shape of the school. *687.563 Courtesy Douglas County History Research Center, Douglas County Libraries.*

Dress Up Day (1938-39). Forty-one children and two teachers pose outside the Sedalia School. The school housed eight grades under one roof with one or two teachers for the entire school. The older four grades had Mr. Wren for their teacher; the lower grades had Mrs. Wiseman. Other elementary schools in the area at the time were Oaklands, Lone Tree, Glen Grove, Indian Park, Jarre Creek and Gann schools. This building was used until 1953 when the new Sedalia Elementary School was built. *Courtesy Louise Beeman Hier.*

Life Goes On (Date unknown). A group of volunteer fire fighters in Sedalia are pictured after helping to put out a big fire. Harriett Beeman, credited with organizing the volunteer fire department, is one of those pictured. Notice how clean everyone looks; the community legend is that everyone went home first to clean up before they had their picture taken. The debris of the fire is in the foreground. The building in the background is the Denver & Rio Grande depot. *687.592 Courtesy Douglas County History Research Center, Douglas County Libraries.*

Theodore Roosevelt Comes to Town (1905). After serving as the Assistant Secretary of the Navy and the Governor of New York, Teddy Roosevelt was nominated for Vice President in 1900, running with President McKinley. McKinley rarely traveled during the election year, but Roosevelt traveled around the country meeting people and gathering votes. His speech in Castle Rock, September 28, 1900, was covered in the newspapers. According to Bertha Manhart's diary, the presidential train pulled into Sedalia on May 8, 1905 and the school children came to see him. *687.523 Courtesy Florence Campbell/Copy at Douglas County History Research Center, Douglas County Libraries.*

Elephant in the Field (Circa 1910). Prior to railroads, the early circuses traveled only as far as the stock horses could pull the wagons. Horses were exhausted after 20 miles on primitive roads. Rail travel offered box and sleeper cars. Traveling 100 miles at night, the circus could now  set up their tent at dawn, march in a parade, offer two performances and move on. This elephant in the fields near the Sedalia school may have been let out of a train to stretch his legs. The school appears as it did before the 1912 addition. *Courtesy Betty Saunders Collection/Copy at Sedalia Historic Fire House Museum.*

Peaceful Train Wreck (Date unknown). Passengers stand next to three derailed Denver & Rio Grande Railroad cars. Derailments were a common occurrence and travel by rail was always an adventure. Special equipment was brought to the site from either Denver or Colorado Springs to put the cars back on the tracks. The two railroads coming through Sedalia were the Denver & Rio Grande Railroad and the Atchison Topeka & Santa Fe Railway. The federal government took over the operation of the railroads in 1917 for the duration of WWI. *Courtesy Betty Saunders collection/Copy at Sedalia Historic Fire House Museum.*

The Great Hunt (1928). Two wagons backed up together with several logs balanced on top, make an excellent way to show off the bounty. Pictured (L to R) are Morgan Roberts, Ray Blunt, Charles Hier, Ed Curtis, Vernon Wyatt, Lloyd Page, Charles Curtis and Nels Anderson. This picture was taken on the Charles Hier ranch. These mule deer were gutted in the field and partially frozen on the trip home. Field dressing, making an incision in the belly of the deer to remove organs and drain blood, preserved the meat until it could be butchered at home. *Courtesy David A. and Carol Curtis.*

The Men Keep Busy Too (Date unknown). Charlie Hier is holding the reins to the horse drawn equipment. The binder was invented in 1872 and was an improvement over the reaper, which only cut the grain. The binder cut the grain and bound it into sheaves using twine. The Hier ranch produced wheat, oats and barley. The farmers stayed busy most of the summer. There were grain elevators in Castle Rock and Littleton to receive the crops. Diesel-powered combines replaced the horse-drawn equipment, making the farmers' work much easier. *Courtesy Louise Beeman Hier.*

The Roaring 20s (Circa 1928). Teenagers, (L to R) Harriett Beeman and Marguerite Morrelli, are having fun posing as flappers or mobsters in front of the local Sedalia Post Office in 1928. From the waist down the girls are wearing skirts, hosiery and dressy shoes. From the waist up they are dressed in men's white shirts with ties and fedoras. The shocking short haircuts also drew attention. The sign on the ground says "Goodrich Tires" and in the window there is an advertisement for a car called the "Overland Six." Albert Manhart was the postmaster at this time. *Courtesy Louise Beeman Hier.*

Burgers But No Fries (December 1949). In December 1949, Bud Hebert opened a new restaurant in Sedalia called "Bud's Bar". The restaurant is famous in Douglas County for its delicious hamburgers and "no French fries" policy. Bud owned the bar until 1964, when he ran for a judgeship in Douglas County and won the election. He could no longer own a bar due to prohibitions for judges, so he sold it to his friend and faithful employee, Therman Thompson. Thompson still owns and manages it. The cars in the picture belong to (left) Sam Burns and (right) Hank Hier. *Courtesy Louise Beeman Hier.*

Chapter Eleven

The Western Region

The Rugged and Beautiful South Platte

by
Laura Adema

The Penley Ranch (Circa 1920). Five miles west of Sedalia lies a beautiful piece of property known as the Penley Ranch. Frank Perry Sobey filed a homestead for part of the land on September 22, 1880. After Sobey's death in 1880, Edward Mortimer Penley acquired the property. Over time, the ranch grew to 1,200 acres, which it remains today. The Penleys have owned and lived on the land for over 125 years. According to Betty O'Neal Francis, in her hand-written history of the Penley family, "The ranch borders the Pike National Forest to the west. Here huge, beautiful deep pink and white rocks rise out of the thickets of oak brush. Tall pines and spruce trees stand guard over the beautiful natural park. Indian Creek flows down through a very rough canyon and past the ranch...several rows of very tall majestic white rocks create a natural entrance to this peaceful spot." The meadow area--the area with all the structures--was once a Ute campground. Wildcat Mountain, the point from which the photograph was taken, was an Native American "look-out." The camera is pointed to the northwest. Roxborough Park lies to the north, which is behind the rocky cliff on the right side. *Courtesy Penley Family Collection.*

English Country Gentleman (Circa 1900). Edward Mortimer Penley (Mortie) was born in Dursley, England in 1858. Mortie's father and brother were both Episcopal priests. His brother Vincent Owen Penley came to Colorado, was ordained, and preached to the mining towns of Trinidad and Idaho Springs. Mortie came to Colorado in 1878 and bought the Sobey Place, southwest of Sedalia, a few years later. Looking for gold, he bought land as far west as Aspen, but he never found any. He named his ranch "Cam Glen" after his boyhood home. His wife, Annie Lapham Penley, was the manager of the ranch. Penley, dressed in the English-country fashion most of the time and preferred his "buggy" to the automobile. *Courtesy Penley Family Collection.*

Start Them Early (Circa 1941). Tom Penley, grandson of Mortimer Penley, sits on a gentle bay named "Sunny." Tom is about five years old. Notice the saddle and short stirrups. The photograph was taken on the Penley Ranch. Children learned to ride horseback

early in those days, or they walked. Tom recalls riding on horseback to Jarre Creek School, a distance of about one and a half miles. When asked how he learned to ride, Tom said, "Well, when I was two or three, I used to ride on the pigs all day and that was my training. After that you just sort of knew." *Courtesy Penley Family Collection.*

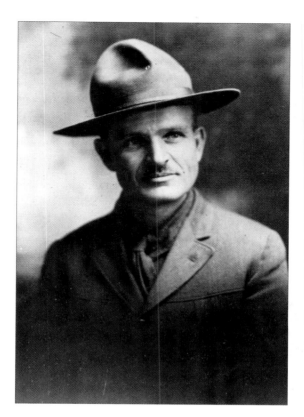

The Lone Forest Ranger (Circa 1920). William (Bill) Kreutzer was the first and longest-serving United States Forest Ranger. On August 8, 1899, at the age of 20, Bill saddled his horse and rode to Denver to interview for the job. He was told by Col. W.T. May to begin work immediately. His territory was 300,000 acres of the Plum Creek Forest Reserve, land that would one day become the Pike National Forest. His pay was $50 per month! Kreutzer was a wiry, five-feet eleven, 165 pound bundle of enthusiasm. He supplied his own horse, food and clothing. The job supplied a bucket, ax, shovel and a map. He returned to his parent's cattle ranch on Indian Creek, west of Sedalia and went to work putting out forest fires. It is difficult today to understand the enormous pressure and lack of support for these early public servants. Forest fires, range wars, illegal land use and protection of property all found their way into Kreutzer's job description. He became a supervisor in 1907, serving in the Gunnison and Roosevelt National Forests. He retired in 1939, with a total of 41 years of service. *Courtesy Richard and Pauline Kreutzer/Copy at Sedalia Historic Fire House Museum.*

How I Spent My Summer (Circa 1919). Helen Dowe grew up in Denver and attended West Side High School. She became a role model for American women when she accepted the position of the first woman "fire lookout" at Devils Head from 1919-22. Her life as a fire lookout was challenging. Lightning was a real threat to her post at 9,300 feet atop Devil's Head. From sunrise to sunset she kept a constant watch on the forest for signs of fire. Other chores included cooking, chopping wood and hauling water. She slept in a log cabin at the base of the steps. *42829A Courtesy US Forest Service.*

View from the top (Circa 1932). In 1907, the US Forest Service planned a series of seven fire lookout stations from Wyoming to New Mexico and Devils Head was one of them. In 1912, the lookout was little more than a tent. In 1919 a small shelter was built. Finally, in 1951 the US Army from Ft. Carson came and enlarged the tower, adding a cabin for the staff. Currently

a one and four-tenths mile trail leads up to the tower with a gain of 948 feet. The panoramic view of the Pike National Forest is worth the climb. *97075.39 Courtesy Douglas County History Research Center, Douglas County Libraries.*

Diamond Jack--Gangster turned Cowboy (Circa 1927). Leland A.Varain, born in 1886, either in Colorado or California, spent his adult life alternating between Chicago gunman and "want-to-be" rancher/cowboy in Jarre Canyon. The Denver Post wrote over 130 stories about Varain between 1922 and 1935. As a legend, the people of Colorado loved him. He wore a big white Stetson hat, drove fancy cars, brandished guns in public places and threw money to the children in the streets. He also wore lots of gaudy diamond jewelry and gave diamonds as gifts. In 1922, he was arrested for stealing $50,000 in jewelry—thus the name Diamond Jack. Another of his aliases was Louis Alterie. The law seemed to cover their eyes at most of Alterie's criminal acts. As a member of the Dion O'Banion gang, Alterie was archrival to Al Capone. On the morning of July 18, 1935, Diamond Jack was gunned down in Chicago on the sidewalk outside of his residence. His wife's life was spared. Gunmen had rented an apartment across the street, waiting for just the right moment. This "rental ambush" was an execution technique Alterie had himself perfected. *X22166 Courtesy Denver Public Library/Copy at Douglas County History Research Center, Douglas Public Libraries.*

The Practice of Forestry (June 1946). "Next to the earth itself, the forest is the most useful servant of man." (A Primer of Forestry, 1905). Soil erosion, fires and wasteful cutting are problems that plagued the first forest rangers. The early settlers had their own ideas about what constituted wise use of the forest; it  was a demand-driven problem. Timber in the early 1900s was needed for railroad ties, mining supports and the building boom in Denver. Notice the "skid" marks, old stumps and erosion in this picture of the Pike National Forest. *440814 Courtesy US Forest Service.*

Everything but the Kitchen Sink (April, 1921). By 1921, an automobile camp and picnic area developed at the base of Devils Head. Denver newspapers lured visitors with glowing reports of the comfortable camping accommodations, fresh air and beautiful views. Helen Dowe, pictured here, attempts to store her gear in the car while the driver remains seated. Her trip to survey forests in southern Colorado was also attended by John Burgess, a surveyor and draftsman for the Forest Service since 1916. The survey was in the Montezuma National Forest. Burgess married Miss Dowe in December of 1921. *153253 Courtesy US Forest Service.*

The Woodbine Girls (July 4, 1938). These young women found summer employment at Woodbine Lodge, located in Jarre Canyon. They wore starched white uniforms and saddle shoes. Pictured are (L to R): Dorothy O'Neal, Gladys McNally, Audrey O'Neal, Rita Rudolph, Louise Beeman and Beulah McManus. Louise (Beeman) Hier remembers her employment as hard work yet fun. The waitresses either lived in rooms above the dining hall or were picked up each day in a touring car. Mornings were spent preparing meals and cleaning. They waited tables in the afternoon and evening. Wages were $1 per day, plus tips. *Courtesy Sedalia Historic Fire House Museum.*

Round Up Ranch (Circa 1924). A group picture shows Round-Up Ranch after a round-up or local rodeo. As the gang wars heated up in Chicago, Louis Alterie, also known as Diamond Jack, made friends and bought property in Colorado. He invited gang leader and friend Dino O'Banion for deer hunting and rodeos in Jarre Canyon. The gang leader

died on November 10, 1924, gunned down in his own flower shop in Chicago. O'Banion is third from the left and Diamond Jack is sixth from the left in the front row. Other Jarre Canyon families in the picture were Carmette, Hall, Buck, Brown and Penley. *Courtesy Castle Rock Museum.*

Indian Park School Drawing (1974). William and Hannah Smith moved to Colorado in 1883, establishing a sawmill in Jarre Canyon. William deeded one acre of land so a school could be built in 1884. It was named Brown School initially; later its name was changed to Indian Park School. On March 19, 1900, Hannah deeded an acre of land for a cemetery. The snows were heavy the year William died; consequently, he was buried behind the school, where a small cemetery exists. This one-room schoolhouse was one of the last to close in Douglas County. There were approximately eight students enrolled during the final term in 1958-59. Heavy snowstorms provided the children with an excuse for snowball fights and sledding near the school. This charming pen and ink drawing of Indian Park School is part of a collection of drawings of one-room schoolhouses, done by talented local artist Mary Love Cornish. Mary, a resident of Jarre Canyon, is the daughter of Charles Waldo Love, a well-know artist and painter. Mary is credited with assembling a visual history entitled "The Schoolhouses of Douglas County." She is an active member of the Indian Park Schoolhouse Association, a group dedicated to preserving the school and cemetery. *Courtesy Mary Love Cornish.*

Foxy Lady (Circa 1928). By the 1920s, fox farming was at its peak in North America, including the farms in Colorado. Black, silver or gray furs were fashionable. Years of selective breeding and good nutrition produced quality pelts like these. In 1913, a pair of breeding silver foxes sold for $25,000. By 1935, overpopulation of foxes drove the price down and women's tastes turned to mink. Many farmers had to let their foxes go, as they couldn't afford to feed them. The woman in the picture is unidentified. *Courtesy of Gail Rocchio-Downes, from the Colorado Silver Fox Company pamphlet.*

Begging for a Raisin (Circa 1928). Roy Crowder feeds a treat to one of his silver foxes. Crowder was superintendent of operations on a fox farm 30 miles south of Denver in Jarre Canyon. The farm was part of The Colorado Silver Fox Company. Silver foxes, or black foxes with silver streaks, are direct descendants of the Charles Dalton line originating in 1895 on Prince Edward Island. Gail Rocchio-Downes now owns part of the "fox farm" land purchased in 1977 by her father, Charles Rocchio. She discovered many fox kennels and pens covering the northern slopes of her property. *Courtesy Gail Rocchio-Downes, from the Colorado Silver Fox Company pamphlet.*

Sprucewood Inn (Circa 1929). In the 1920s, Walter Barth from Denver, also known as the "Carnation King," bought thousands of acres of investment property west of Sedalia. Barth, the owner of several greenhouses in Englewood, Colorado, built a three-room wood frame house and several cabins to be used as a summer resort at the Y-junction of Highway 67 at Nighthawk Hill and Sugar Creek Road. One of the cabins was used as a school for local children. Also in the 1920s the house was jacked up and a larger log cabin was constructed underneath. Barth ran a general store there until the crash of 1929. He leased the property to the grandparents of George Ehnes in the 40s and 50s. In the 70s George Ehnes was able to buy the property and ran a towing service, emergency fire and rescue and a snow plowing operation. George and Sharon Melvin bought the Sprucewood Inn in 1984, continuing the bar and restaurant, but adding the dimension of a community gathering place. Neighbors gather to eat, drink and listen to music. Occasional potluck dinners are served as a social event. The Sprucewood Inn is one of the few remaining restaurants along Highway 67 between Sedalia and Woodland Park. *Courtesy George and Sharon Melvin.*

West Creek or Bust (February 25, 1896). The story of West Creek begins in 1895 when George F. Tyler sent his sons to Denver with ore samples from his ranch. Initial test results showed some gold, with lesser amounts of silver, lead, iron, copper and platinum. The gold rush was on. Local legend says the first gold was "salted" or planted, in a scheme to sell land. By January 1896, The Daily News in Denver called West Creek "the largest mining district in the state." Several campsites around West Creek including Pemberton and Tyler decided to unite and incorporate as one town. On March 16, 1896, West Creek became the second incorporated town in Douglas County. The first was Castle Rock. In January of that year the population was around 500. One month later it had doubled. Never was public confidence as high regarding the outlook for the mines of West Creek. The picture shows horse-drawn carts filled with ore. Unfortunately, the ore near the surface was soon depleted. Another method, hard rock mining, yielded similar bleak results. By 1897, there were less than 100 people remaining where 1200 had thrived a year before. *654.16 Courtesy Douglas County History Research Center, Douglas County Libraries.*

H-316 Cottages, Deckers Springs, Colo. 1920's

First Daffodil--Then Deckers (Circa 1920). The locale of Deckers was originally known as Daffodil until it took the name of a local businessman, Stephen A. Decker. Decker was a railroad man who first settled a mining claim in the area, but when no gold was discovered, turned his attention to building a saloon and a general store. Cottages were built to accommodate visitors who came to fish and drink from the Lithia spring that ran behind the general store. In 1897, realizing the curative effects of the spring water, Mr. Decker traveled to Denver to speak with physicians to persuade them to encourage their patients to make a visit. As mentioned in *Echoes of Forgotten Places* by Nell Fletcher, some physicians asserted, "Within forty-five miles of Denver was a mineral spring superior to the famous one at Carlsbad." Eventually, 27 buildings were built in and around the resort to accommodate guests. Transportation was an issue, but it was noted in a pamphlet published by The Bradford Publishing Co. that a stage would meet "...all morning trains at South Platte, and by notifying Mr. Decker in advance, his private conveyance will always be found at the railway station...." *Courtesy Mountain Artisans Arts Council.*

Catch of the Day (1924). This unidentified young woman wearing riding breeches and leather boots holds her catch of "speckled beauties" (trout). The notation on the photograph states "1924 Fishing one week end near Deckers." A pamphlet called "The Deckers Mineral Resort," published by The Bradford Publishing Co., Denver, Colorado, lured fishermen with "...the South Platte is fairly alive with the speckled beauties and untold thousands of small fry are added each year, which assures an inexhaustible supply of fish of regulation size." Visitors arrived at the resort not only to fish, but also to take advantage of the medicinal spring that runs behind the store. The pamphlet also advertised that Deckers had "the only Lithia Baths in the U.S." As news spread, the resort became popular for those seeking a cure for many diseases. Dr. C.B. Richmond said of the mineral waters, "I am pleased to state that I have used water from Deckers' mineral springs, and in many cases of functional troubles with digestive and urinary tracts it has done more good...that I truly believe that these springs are destined to become among the most noted in the world." *Courtesy Douglas County History Research Center, Douglas County Libraries*

The Way it Was (March 24, 1899). The town of Trumbull first appeared as a gold camp in 1896 and later became a fishing resort. The town straddles the South Platte River. The best fishing is rumored to be on the Jefferson County side. The river is behind the buildings and Long Scraggy looms in the center of the photograph. Only the hillside on the right belongs to Douglas County. About 20 buildings remain, two or three on the Douglas County side and the rest in Jefferson County. It no longer appears on any Colorado state map. *Courtesy Mountain Artisans Arts Council.*

Cowboying On The Platte (Circa 1948). (L to R): Bill Benight on Stranger, Jack Wilcox (on an unnamed steed) and Lou (Bud) Fletcher on Buster. Speedy the dog stands behind Lou Fletcher's paint. The Fletcher Ranch, near Deckers, now comprises three 80 acre portions that stair step along Horse Creek. Lou was only one-year old in 1933 when his father purchased the ranch. Lou's father asked the Siebert boy, then ten years old, if he hated to move. The reply was "Shoot, no! Dad says a big flood is going to come along and wash the whole shootin' match away anyhow." *Courtesy Lou and Nell Fletcher.*

Bridge Above Strontia Springs (Circa 1912). The Denver South Park & Pacific Railroad tracks curved through the South Platte River Canyon. The steep walls of sheer granite and huge boulders at the river's edge amazed travelers. Two iron trestles, or bridges, carried the train from one side of the canyon wall to the other, traveling on one edge of the river, which was Douglas County, then over the bridge to the other side, which was Jefferson County. A total distance of eight and one half miles of track was constructed through the narrow, twisted canyon. The bridge pictured was called the Deansbury Bridge, later renamed the Strontia Springs Bridge. The resort and rail station of Deansbury was named for C.A. Deane who furnished all the ties for the canyon rail line. Thirty thousand ties were simply floated down the river and then lifted out using heavy booms. The rest were hauled on flatbed cars. More than 100,000 ties came from the Deane lumber camp. In some places, the roadbed was supported on retaining walls, in others blasted out of solid granite. A dam, constructed in Waterton Canyon, was completed in 1982. The area called Strontia Springs is submerged under the reservoir. *Courtesy Colorado Railroad Museum Collection.*

Known for the Cuisine. (Date unknown). So many visitors arrived in the town of South Platte, first called Symes, that an entrepreneurial man, who owned the Zang Brewing Company in Denver, decided to build a luxury hotel called the South Platte Hotel in 1877. He relocated one of his bartenders from Denver, Charlie Walbrecht, to run the day-to-day operation. "Mata," who had been a personal cook of the Zang's, arrived to run the kitchen. Soon the hotel gained a reputation for the wonderful food Mata prepared. This early photograph clearly shows the railroad tracks of the Denver, South Park and Pacific Railroad. A special "fish train" ran on the weekends. *Courtesy Colorado Railroad Museum Collection.*

Cheesman Lake Boat House and Cottages (July 1905). Local fishermen thought the water from the Cheesman Dam was ruining fishing on the South Platte River. The Water Board published a brochure in September 1934 stating "The water needed from Lake Cheesman to replenish operating reservoirs in and about Denver usually is not sent down the Platte until dark on Sunday nights during the fishing season, so as

not to hinder fishing in any avoidable way." These cottages and boathouse must have been built for the employees who operated the valves and broke up ice floes on the lake, since fishing or trespassing on private property was illegal. *Courtesy Denver Board of Water Commissioners.*

Million Dollar Dam (July 1905). The Cheesman Reservoir, pictured above, is Colorado's third largest water storage facility. Completed in January 1905, it has an 18-mile shoreline and a 79,000 acre foot water capacity. The curved arch of granite blocks is 210 feet tall, built just below the juncture of Goose Creek and the south fork of the South Platte River in southwestern Douglas County. The Denver Union Water Company, formed in 1894, and its president, Walter S. Cheesman, are credited with construction of the dam. Cheesman came to Denver in 1894 to operate a drug store and became interested in railroads, real estate and the Denver water supply. The project was constructed in less than five years, in a formidable canyon area, from granite blocks weighing up to 11 tons and in the same general area as the Goose Creek Dam. That dam had the misfortune of busting loose in a spring flood in 1900, destroying railroad tracks, bridges and other structures in its path down the Platte River. Public outcry over the easily demolished dam and determination of the engineers led to a beautiful new million-dollar dam. The caption below the picture says, "Mr. Cheesman and family in the boat." *Courtesy Denver Board of Water Commissioners.*

The Authors

Laura Adema

Laura, a registered nurse and freelance writer, has lived in Colorado since 1971. She moved to Castle Rock with her husband in 1999. A native of Michigan, she grew up in Grand Rapids, where she loved both reading and writing. She was the editor of her high school newspaper and joined the Army after graduation from nursing school. She is a member of the Castle Rock Writers, New Hope Writers and the American Christian Writers. She writes articles for local newspapers and newsletters on topics related to nursing, local history and human-interest.

Alice Aldridge-Dennis

Alice Aldridge-Dennis, freelance writer and former English teacher, explored the West early on, from the back of her family's station wagon. A St. Louis native, she moved here 12 years ago with her husband and two sons. She brought Midwestern enthusiasm to church life, the PTA, and Boy Scouts. She now reports for the Castle Rock Daily Star. Holding a B.A. in English and an M.S. in communications, Aldridge-Dennis is a member of the Society of Professional Journalists, Phi Kappa Phi, and the National Council of Teachers of English. Locally, she belongs to Castle Rock Writers and New Hope Writers. She is the moderator of Presbyterian Women for the Presbytery of Denver.

Derald E. Hoffman

Derald, a native of Luther, Iowa, first taught in the Nike Guided-Missile School at Fort Bliss, Texas, then 30 years with Littleton Public Schools and now in the Scottsdale and Fountain Hills schools. He and his wife live in Castle Rock, Colorado, during the summer and Fountain Hills, Arizona, during the winter. He is a member of the Castle Rock Writers, New Hope Writers, a chaplain of American Legion Post 1187 and Docent at the River of Time Museum. He is a freelance writer, photographer, videographer and digital camera instructor. He has organized and taken groups to Washington D.C., Europe, Russia, China and Zimbabwe. His photographs and articles have appeared in local newspapers.

Susan Koller

Susan moved to Colorado over 10 years ago with her family, after living in three Midwestern states they are here to stay. Susan is a columnist for the Perry Park Sentinel and an author of short stories, three family history books and poetry. She is also a member of the Castle Rock Writers Group, the Larkspur Historical Society and the Douglas County Historic Preservation Board. Susan teaches sewing at the Larkspur Elementary School in their After School Enrichment program, and is helping with the Larkspur Historical Society's web site. She also loves quilting, gardening, photography, and archeology. Susan is now building a custom clothing business with the help of a friend.

Kathleen Stevens McCoy

Kathleen is from Maryland and moved to Colorado with her husband and two daughters in the 1980s. She has a degree in communications, but spent most of her career as a dental hygienist. She played violin with the South Suburban Community Orchestra for nine years and now performs with the Castle Rock Town Band. She enjoys being outdoors in beautiful Douglas County riding her quarter horse, Leo. As an original member of the Castle Rock Writers, she learned to record oral histories and volunteers this service in the community.

Marjorie Meyerle

Marjorie has taught Advanced Placement English for three school districts, two in Colorado and one in Northern Virginia. She is a fiction writer and three-time recipient of fellowships at the Virginia Center for the Creative Arts and three scholarships to the Bread Loaf Writers' Conference in Middlebury, VT. She placed in the 1986 Writer's Digest Writing Competition with her literary short story, "Latch Key Child." She has three grown sons and lives with her husband, a corporate attorney for Time-Warner Cable, in Franktown, Colorado. She is a member and docent for the Franktown and Parker Historical Societies.

Susan Trumble

Roxborough has had a special place in Susan's heart since she first saw it in 1976. After completing a Bachelor's and Master's Degrees in Natural Resource Management at Colorado State University, she was employed by Colorado State Parks. One of her first assignments was to work with the team planning Roxborough State Park. Later she was appointed the park manager and served in that capacity for 22 years. Douglas County has been her home since 1982. Currently a stay-at-home mom, she dedicates time to Roxborough State Park and the Douglas County Historical Preservation Board.

Elizabeth Wallace

Elizabeth, born and educated in England, is a member of the Society of Women Writers and Journalists in London. In 1978, she emigrated to the United States with her husband and three young sons. A founding member of the Castle Rock Writers, she is very active in the local literary community. Elizabeth has authored three books: Extraordinary Places...Close to London; Colorado Springs, Colorado; and Kansas City in Vintage Postcards. Elizabeth writes a weekly newspaper column, gives guest speaking addresses, and appears on radio and television to discuss her books and topics of interest. Her favorite topics are etymology, historical events, and unique travel experiences. Elizabeth is currently working on her first novel.

Linda M. Grey

Linda was born in New Haven, CT. She obtained her degree in Medical Technology from Salve Regina College in Rhode Island. She relocated to Colorado in June 2001 with her husband and two children. Linda demonstrated the heart of a writer before she even put pen to paper. An intuitive person, Linda wrote beautiful letters to friends and co-workers filled with encouragement and praise. She also wrote letters to the editor and government representatives. Her other interests included photography and hiking. A member of the Castle Rock Writers, she served as the original editor of the Douglas County book project. She provided leadership and shared her extensive research of Douglas County with her fellow writers.